# The Jyotirlingas



PRAISE FOR THE BOOK

'A great writer in the making, Samhitha Reddy has unleashed her creativity with full force. I appreciate the attempt and recommend the work to all readers.'
– Sri M, spiritual guide

A bibliophile and dendrophile, **Samhitha** is an Indian lawyer who navigates the intricate worlds of international human rights and development with passion and purpose. An avid traveller, she immerses herself in diverse cultures and cuisines, all while indulging in her love for Indian mythology and history. Whether she is crafting compelling narratives to champion causes close to her heart or savouring local delicacies in hidden cafés, Samhitha's adventures are always a mix of curiosity, compassion and boundless wanderlust.

ANCIENT INDIAN TEMPLES

# The Jyotirlingas

## TALES OF THE TWELVE SHRINES

Samhitha Reddy

hachette INDIA

First published in 2024 by Hachette India
(Registered name: Hachette Book Publishing India Pvt. Ltd)
An Hachette UK company
www.hachetteindia.com

SRD


Illustrations by Neelima P Aryan
Section dividers and frame corners from Vecteezy.com
Temple illustrations on pages 192 to 219 from Shutterstock.com



ISBN 978-93-5731-619-4

Hachette Book Publishing India Pvt. Ltd
4th & 5th Floors, Corporate Centre
Plot No. 94, Sector 44, Gurugram – 122003, India

Typeset by Manmohan Kumar, Delhi

Printed and bound in India
by Manipal Technologies Limited

FSC
www.fsc.org
MIX
Paper | Supporting responsible forestry
FSC™ C043100

For anyone who has ever marvelled at the beauty of Indian temples and ruminated on the myths that breathe life into their stones

THE JYOTIRLINGAS
KEDARESHWAR
VISHWESHWAR
MAHAKALESHWAR
BAIDYANATH
NAGESHWAR
OMKARESHWAR
SOMNATH
GRISHNESHWAR
TRAYAMBAKESHWAR
BHIMASHANKAR
BAY OF BENGAL
MALLIKARJUNA
ARABIAN SEA
RAMESHWAR
INDIAN OCEAN

# CONTENTS

*One day of Brahma has fourteen Indras*
*His lifetime has fifty-four thousand Indras*
*One day of Vishnu is the lifetime of Brahma*
*The lifetime of Vishnu is one day of Shiva*
– from the *Shiva Purana*

*Saurashtre Somanatham cha Shrishaile Mallikarjunam*
*Ujjeyinyam Mahakalam Omkaram-Amaleshwaram*
*Paralyam Vaidyanatham cha Dakinyam Bhimashankaram*
*Setubandhe tu Ramesham Nagesham Darukavane*
*Varanasyam tu Vishweshwam Tryambakam Gautami-tate*
*Himalaye tu Kedaram Ghushmesham cha Shivalaye*
*Etani jyotirlingani sayam pratah patthennarah*
*Sapta-janma-krtam papam smaranena vinashyati*

Somanath in Saurashtra, Mallikarjuna in Srisailam
Mahakal in Ujjain, Omkaram in Amaleshwar
Vaidyanath in Parali, Bhimashankar in the South
Rameshwar near the bridge in Setu, Nageshwar in the Daruka forest
Vishweshwar in Varanasi, Trayambakeshwar on the shores of the Godavari
Kedareshwar in the Himalayas, and Ghushmesha in Shivalaya
He who remembers them, morning and evening
Would wash away sins, committed in his seven births.

# PREFACE

The *Shiva Purana* is the foundational source for all things Mahadeva. It is the narration of the glory of Mahadeva by Sage Suta to a group of brahmins. It is from this ancient text that I derived the inspiration for the stories rendered in this collection.

The stories of the origin of the *jyotirlingas* are contained in the chapter titled '*Kotirudra Samhitha*' of the *Shiva Purana*. The brahmins ask Suta-ji to describe the chronicles of the *jyotirlingas*; explaining how they came into existence and their significance: 'Shiva is *saguna*, that is, with form. But He is also *nirguna*, meaning without qualities or form. And so, the phallic structure, that is the *lingam*, describes our Lord perfectly: all-pervading and omnipresent without the manifestation of His form.'

Suta-ji elucidates that the phallic structures of Shiva on earth and in the Universe are limitless, transcending boundaries. Shiva, a numinous and infinite being, embodies a presence that extends beyond quantifiable measures. However, he declares, 'I shall regale you with the tales of the inception of some of the most revered phallic structures of Shiva. O Brahmins, Shiva is worshipped across the three worlds by the *devas, asuras* and *manavas* alike. He appears before the most ardent of His devotees when they are in the direst of situations and manifests Himself as the phallic form after carrying out the crucial task of their preservation and protection.

Suta-ji says: 'He presents Himself in this form as a remembrance to all His devotees of the difficult times they had once faced. His objective for taking the form in the three worlds is to be accessible to those who seek Him and those who wish to worship Him on their journey to salvation.'

And so, Suta-ji narrates the sublime and enchanting tales of the *jyotirlingas*, transporting listeners to a realm of mystical wonder and awe.

# PROLOGUE

Eons ago. . .

During the initial *shveta varaha kalpa*, six sages gathered at the Triveni Sangam, where the mighty Ganga, the elegant Yamuna and the mystical Saraswati converge in sacred harmony, and began debating who the greatest deity of all was: Brahma, Vishnu or Maheshwara? Unable to settle the debate, the six approached Lord Brahma himself.

Lord Brahma pronounced, 'O revered sages! The source of Vishnu, Rudra and all the deities, including myself, and all other creations, is none other than Mahadeva. Union with Shiva should be the objective of every person. Listening to His qualities, singing devotional songs in His praise and contemplating on Him are the greatest means that help one to unite with Him.'

# THE BIRTH
## of the Lingam

In the first *shveta varaha kalpa,* Lord Brahma decided to visit Lord Vishnu.

The Preserver's paradisical abode was *vaikuntha loka,* an unparalleled sanctuary of opulence and resplendence, studded with grand palaces adorned with intricately crafted pillars and domes embellished with a dazzling array of precious gemstones. This sacred expanse, encompassing diverse *janapadas*, was exclusively attainable by the purest of souls. Vast, verdant gardens extended as far as the eye could behold, boasting an exquisite assortment of flora and fauna beyond mere mortal imagination. The heavenly fragrance of the ethereal blooms enveloped visitors from the moment they crossed the threshold, immersing them in the intoxicating allure of all the wonders that *vaikuntha loka* had to offer.

On reaching Lord Vishnu's abode, Lord Brahma discovered him lying on Sheshanaga, being attended to by Garuda and a flock of his other attendants. Sheshanaga, the king of serpents, looked majestic as he floated effortlessly on his innumerable coils in the Ocean of Milk or *kshirasagara*, his five arched heads forming a magnificent canopy over his Lord's form as he lay resting. Garuda, the king of birds, lay at his Lord's feet, a symbol of devout servitude. Part-human and part-eagle, this majestic beast was the Preserver's vehicle of choice or *vahana*, as they said in *vaikuntha*.

The blue-skinned deity exuded an aura of tranquillity as he reclined, his almond-shaped eyes half open, and his features radiating a serene rhapsody. The sweet fragrance of lotus, the Creator's favourite scent, gently wafted through the air.

In just a few fleeting moments of Lord Brahma's arrival, a surging wave of anger swept over him as Lord Vishnu, in his undisturbed repose, made no effort to awaken or greet him.

Swallowing his initial anger, Lord Brahma proceeded towards Sheshanaga, where Lord Vishnu lay comfortably. Unperturbed and adorned with an untroubled smile, Lord Vishnu remained reclined on the majestic serpent, lazily observing as the Creator of the Universe approached him, the air ripe with reckoning of what was to come.

'Greetings, my Lord!' the Creator said sarcastically as he suppressed his pride and feigned a bow.

'And to you, my Lord! What brings you to my humble abode?' Vishnu enquired nonchalantly, still showing no intention of rising.

That was the breaking point for Brahma. He was unable to tolerate the perceived disrespect any longer, and his eyes tightened to narrow slits of seething hostility. Such discourtesy! And the audacity! How could someone, even Lord Vishnu, fail to extend a polite greeting to the Creator of the Universe, he thought to himself, as he took note of Vishnu's dismissive demeanour. Livid, standing across the still lounging Vishnu, he thundered, 'Such insolence! Do you consider yourself superior to me? Is your self-centredness so extreme that you cannot rise to greet your peer respectfully, as befitting of my stature?'

Startled by the incensed voice, Vishnu sat up, his eyes wide, just as Sheshanaga too slowly opened his ten eyes and Garuda looked up from his reverie to see who had the courage to raise their voice against their Lord. 'After all, he is the Preserver of the Universe,' they thought to themselves.

'Do not raise your voice at me, O Lord. Regardless of the cause of your anger, we can discuss it in a more amicable manner! I did not deem it necessary to rise and greet a peer whom I also consider a friend. Moreover, I had not taken note of your arrival until you addressed me!'

Vishnu's words failed to pacify Brahma, fuelling his anger instead. Peer or not, how could someone, even a friend, fail to offer him, the great Brahma, greetings? Indignation surged within him. And just like that, Vishnu too became irritated by the demand for self-proclaimed supremacy and Brahma's arrogant demeanour.

This disagreement escalated into a heated argument, exploding into a barrage of verbal exchanges, ultimately culminating in a showdown of all-powerful arms.

The Creator and the Preserver unsheathed their formidable weapons, charging at each other with a force that reverberated through the heavens. The clash between the latter's weapons, the *Kaumodaki* and the

*Sudharshana Chakra*, and the former's primary weapon, the *Brahmashira Astra*, sent shockwaves across the three *lokas*, causing violent tremors that left all living beings trembling in fear for their lives, unable to discern the trigger for the very ground shaking beneath them.

In a conflict of epic proportions, the powerful adversaries – Vishnu, mounted on Garuda who was now just as irked as his Lord, and Brahma, mounted on his white swan, Hamsa – fought ferociously, aiming their most deadly and potent *astras* and unleashing them at each other with the precision of the seasoned warriors they were.

The onlooking *devas* grew increasingly anxious as the protracted battle showed no signs of abating, with neither the Creator nor the Preserver showing symptoms of tiring. Not even a single drop of sweat appeared on their mighty brows, while the severity of each attack exponentially increased. With each thunderous blow exchanged, the foreheads of the spectators furrowed with worry while their worlds quaked violently. The gravity of the situation became increasingly apparent – unless a solution was found to halt these equally matched opponents, the very fabric of existence would unravel and descend into devastating chaos, and the peaceful, joyous life they had known would come to an unfortunate end.

Seated in their softly cushioned golden chariots, the *devas* felt their hearts gripped by fear. Terror filled their eyes as they witnessed the cataclysmic conflict. The two Lords of the Universe's holy Trinity, locked in a relentless struggle, remained oblivious to the widespread destruction unfolding in the worlds around them – which one meticulously created, and the other ardently preserves.

Worrying for the safety of their dominion as well as the rest of the Universe, a congregation of the *deva*s approached Lord Shiva. They meant to tell Him about the matter at hand, beseeching Him to intervene and bring an end to the ongoing tumultuous battle. Mahadeva, ever-omniscient and omnipresent, was aware of the unfolding events. Indeed, He too could feel the tremors in His icy abode, Kailasha.

His body adorned with ash, a serpent around His neck, a crescent moon on His matted hair, the sacred Ganga flowing down from His wild matted locks to the depths of the world, Mahadeva held His trident, the *trishul*, in one hand, the other resting in His lap, palm open upwards. He slowly opened His all-seeing eyes, as if awakening from a peaceful sleep, choosing to keep His third eye on His forehead shut as the ongoing pandemonium did not call for destruction of any sort. Yet.

Feigning ignorance, with a slight smile on His lips, Mahadeva looked at the *deva*s questioningly as they hurried towards Him with distress etched on their faces. 'What is the matter, my dear *deva*s? Is something bothering your merry, luxurious existence in *swarga*?' He asked, mischief twinkling in His eyes.

'*Pranam,* Mahadeva!' they cried as they fell at His feet.

One *deva* intimated Him of the fierce battle between Lord Brahma and Lord Vishnu – a conflict born from a minor disagreement, now threatening the entirety of the Universe.

Another added, shuddering if not because of the cold, then due to the thought of the possible outcome of the confrontation without the intervention of a higher power, 'They are so consumed by their escalating fury towards each other that they have become utterly oblivious to the cataclysmic repercussions of their discord on the Universe.'

'If they continue even for a little while longer, all the three worlds will be completely annihilated in the way of collateral damage.'

'Please, O Lord! We humbly beg you to intervene and protect not just us, but the entire three worlds and the very Universe itself.'

'Your Esteemed Holiness is the only being in existence who can save us from total annihilation!'

'Please intervene now, O Mahadeva! Please be so kind as to save us all.'

Mahadeva patiently listened on as each *deva* took turns pleading and imploring that He save the three worlds, with a serene, sagacious smile playing on His face, aglow with a warm ethereal light. He chuckled under His breath as He let slip a white *ketaki* bloom from His thick knotted locks of matted hair. . .

Once the *devas* had each said their piece, Mahadeva sat silently in serene contemplation amid the icy splendour of Kailasha. As though He did not already know what He had planned to do to abate His peers' furies, He nodded to indicate that their desperate pleas had reached His ears.

Mahadeva said, 'Do not worry, O *devas*. The Universe and all the beings in it are just as precious to me as they are to you. I will not let everything be destroyed just because of a squabble between my dear Vishnu and Brahma. Please return to your dwellings, and rest assured that I shall address your concerns and settle the dispute between the two.'

Pacified by the reassuring words of Mahadeva, the *devas* bowed deeply in veneration to the Destroyer and returned to their abodes.

Aware of the gravity of the situation, Lord Shiva decided to visit the scene of the transversal conflict.

Nandi, His *vahana*, stood majestically by the gates of Kailasha, patiently waiting for his Lord to avail his services. His pure and lustrous white coat glistened in the sunlight, in concord with the snow-laden mountains around him.

With His consort, Parvati, by His side, Mahadeva rode Nandi to the battleground, where the clash between Lord Brahma and Lord Vishnu was about to reach its zenith. The winds of the Universe carried whispers of unease. The heavens themselves seemed to hold their breath as the Lord of Destruction prepared to restore intergalactic peace and harmony.

Upon arriving, He saw that both Lord Brahma and Vishnu were ready to unleash their most potent weapons against each other, the *Maheshwarastra* and *Pashupatastra* respectively. The two deities faced each other with visages contorted in anger, their seraphic expressions marred by the intensity of their wrath. Having inflicted and sustained multiple aggressive blows, the two were on the verge of releasing their final weapons.

Mindful of the extreme obliteration that such an action could cause, Lord Shiva finally decided to intervene. Just as the two warring gods released their *astras*, He manifested Himself as an *antalstambha* (pillar of fire) between them. The deadly weapons were engulfed by the *antalstambha* on release, and were consequently destroyed. Neither of the warring celestials had noticed His arrival or intervention.

The *antalstambha* stood tall and one could neither see where the column of fire began nor ended. As the inferno raged, sparks danced in every direction, a mesmerizing display of searing heat that had engulfed the deadliest weapons. The *devas* stood witness, spellbound by the apotheosized phenomenon unfolding before their eyes.

The Creator and the Preserver were taken aback by the sudden appearance of a towering mast of fire before them. Momentarily forgetting their animosity, they exchanged questioning glances as they began to realize that neither of them had caused this sudden occurrence.

'What is that?' Brahma asked, stupefied.

'I have no idea – this is not something I have witnessed before!' Vishnu responded, equally perplexed.

'I have never seen any object or being that had the power to withstand any of my weapons,' Brahma exclaimed, shock and awe evident in his voice. 'And this blazing pillar has simultaneously enveloped both of our devastating weapons as if it was nothing!'

'We have to find out the origin of this pillar of fire!' Vishnu declared with a sense of urgency. 'I am going to seek its head in the skies, you search for its base in the ground.'

The mysterious pillar of fire demanded immediate investigation. An unspoken, temporary truce was established, just as swiftly as the battle had commenced.

The Creator transformed himself into a swan and flew high up into the sky, determined to fathom the extent of the summit of the *antalstambha.* Similarly, the Preserver transformed himself into a boar and hastened to *patala loka* to the foundation of the pillar.

The higher Brahma flew, the more elusive the top of the pillar seemed, as if it had no end. Vishnu faced the same predicament down below. The further he descended, the deeper the pillar lengthened, endlessly, before his eyes. Both deities, confronted with the impossibility of discerning the pillar's boundaries, eventually returned from their fruitless endeavours, agitated, belligerent and confused.

On his way back, Lord Brahma encountered a seductive fragrance immediately captivating his senses.

Brahma could not resist inquiring about the origin of this enchanting bloom. 'O flower of hypnotic fragrance! Where do you come from? I have never seen nor smelt a floret like you before.'

The *ketaki* flower responded, 'Dear Lord, I have been falling since the beginning of time itself. I have no memory of how or when I was born, or how long I have been falling. All I know is that I have been falling along this great pillar of fire ever since I can remember.' The flower also cautioned Lord Brahma against attempting to discover the limit of the pillar, deeming it a futile endeavour. 'I have not reached the base of this majestic pillar of fire yet. How do you plan on finding the extremity, dear Lord?' the flower inquired.

Without hesitation, Brahma proposed, 'Dear flowerette, please assist me. I will take you back with me, and I will tell Vishnu that I was able to reach the top of this pillar of fire. You agree with me and tell him that you saw me reaching its tip.'

The flower, however, advised against deceit, urging Brahma to speak the truth. 'Dear Lord, you must not lie about it. Why do you not just tell the truth? Only harm will come of lying!'

In a state of exasperation and impatience, Brahma replied to the *ketaki* blossom, 'O flower, Vishnu has treated me with disrespect. I wish to surpass him and put him in his place. He has descended below to seek the foundation of this pillar. Just as I could not find the top, I am sure he has failed to find the bottom. I beg of you, please endorse my declaration.' With these words, Brahma took the beautiful blossom back with him.

Upon his return, Brahma witnessed a dejected Vishnu waiting for him. 'Alas, I was unable to find the foundation of this mysterious pillar of fire,' sighed Vishnu.

Brahma emitted a mirthless laugh and smugly announced, 'Yet, I was able to reach the pinnacle of this pillar of fire. This *ketaki* flower saw me do so.' The sprig remained silent, neither confirming nor denying Brahma's claim.

Meanwhile, Lord Vishnu, acknowledging the supposed superiority of Lord Brahma, bowed at his feet as Brahma revelled in his triumph.

Enraged by the deceptive actions of Lord Brahma, Lord Shiva manifested Himself in a majestic display of empyrean wrath. Emerging from the pillar, He stood in His complete glory, His eyes blazing with an intensity that mirrored the might of His anger. In His hand, He held the *trishul*, a potent symbol of His infinite power. Adorned in a tiger-skin loincloth, His formidable presence was accentuated by the coils of His favourite serpent wrapped around His neck, a symbol of His dominance over the serpent world.

As He addressed the assembly of gods, Mahadeva's voice carried the weight of authority, echoing through the dimensions. Vishnu, in awe of His majestic form, observed with deep admiration, recognizing the entrancing force that stood before him. In stark contrast, Brahma experienced guilt and remorse for his wrongdoing, heralding the weight of the consequences to come.

Mahadeva focused His fiery gaze towards Brahma and severed the head that had lied to Vishnu. The five-headed Brahma now only had four. Mahadeva then directed His gaze towards Vishnu to acknowledge the unflinching honesty of the Preserver. He proclaimed, 'You have been truthful throughout this ordeal and so living beings shall always worship you freely. You will be worshipped just as much as I am.'

Then, shifting back His focus to Brahma with stern authority, Shiva cast a lasting judgement upon the Creator. Brahma, the one who had resorted to a lie, was condemned to a fate devoid of worship. He decreed, 'Neither will Brahma be worshipped again, nor will he ever have a temple built in his name. Let this be the mark of his lies for all eternity!'

The wrath of Mahadeva extended even to the *ketaki* flower, a witness to Brahma's deception. The flower, forever tainted by its role in the manufacture of falsehood, was cursed by Him. Henceforth, the *ketaki* would be barred from being offered for any form of worship. These momentous proclamations became enduring reminders of the consequences of deception and the power of truth in the deific order.

Brahma, overcome with shame, prostrated before Lord Shiva, seeking forgiveness. Brahma's plea assuaged Shiva's anger. He declared that Lord Brahma would be the presiding deity for all *yagnas* henceforth, and the *ketaki* flower received the fortune of being offered to Lord Vishnu for worship. The Creator and the Preserver then humbly bowed before Lord Shiva.

This event marked the first time they worshipped Lord Shiva, celebrated as *Shivratri,* an auspicious occasion that marked the birth of the *lingam.*

## The Twelve Jyotirlingas

The *jyotirlingas* stand as revered conduits of divine energy, forming an integral aspect of the worship of Lord Shiva. Each one, a sacred embodiment of the Supreme essence, radiates a celestial aura that draws devotees towards the heart of spiritual commitment. These phallic structures transcend the earthly sphere, and are believed to be a manifestation of Lord Shiva Himself.

Visiting any of these sacred places of worship is believed to grant the wishes of the pilgrims and cleanse them of all sins. Simply listening to the chanting of the names of the twelve *jyotirlingas* is said to fulfil every desire – provided one listens with a pure heart and a clean mind – freeing the individual from the cyclical burden of karma in the Hindu belief of life, death and rebirth. There are sixty-four *jyotirlingas* in all, but twelve of these are considered to be the most auspicious, namely:

- Somnath in Saurashtra, Gujarat
- Mallikarjuna in Srisailam, Andhra Pradesh

- Mahakaleshwar in Ujjain, Madhya Pradesh
- Omkareshwar/Amreshwar in Omkar, Madhya Pradesh
- Kedareshwar in the Himalayas, Uttarakhand
- Bhimashankar on the bank of the River Bhima, Maharashtra
- Vishweshwar in Varanasi, Uttar Pradesh
- Trayambakeshwar on the bank of the River Gautami, Maharashtra
- Baidyanath in Chitabhumi, Jharkhand
- Nageshwar, situated between Darukavana and Bhet Dwarka, Gujarat
- Rameshwar in Betubandh, Tamil Nadu
- Grishneshwar in Shivalaya, Maharashtra

Together, the twelve *jyotirlingas* are also referred to as *dvadasha jyotirlingas*. Their significance is that they are *swayambhu* or self-manifested *lingams*. Each of these formidable phallic structures is believed to have originated as a result of Mahadeva taking the form of the *lingam* to bless us with His eternal presence on earth in these select holy spots.

The above-mentioned *jyotirlingas* are associated with an *upalinga* (ancillary phallic structure) each. According to the *Shiva Purana*, while some of the locations are unknown, the following ancillary *lingas* are known to us:

- Antakesh from Someshwar at the confluence of the River Mahi and the Arabian Sea
- Rudreshwar from Mallikarjuna at Bharukaccha
- Dughdeshwar from Mahakal along the River Narmada

- Kardameshwar from Amreshwar in the vicinity of the Bindu Lake, considered to be a source of seven rivers in the Himalayas
- Bhuteshwar from Kedareshwar, on the banks of the River Yamuna
- Bhimeshwar from Bhimashankar, situated in the Sahya mountains
- Bhuteshwar from Nageshwar, on the banks of the rivers Mallika and Saraswati
- Gupteshwar from Rameshwar
- Vyagreshwar from Grishneshwar

The *jyotirlingas* not only have mythological, religious, cultural and historical significance but are also considered to have scientific implications. It is believed that the structures of these temples take into consideration natural vibrations and energy flow factors, aligning with the energy points of our bodies, thus offering a sense of peace to our anatomy and physiology.

# SOMNATH
## The Curse of the Waxing and Waning Moon

*Saurashtra-deshe vishade-tiramye*
*Jyotirmayam chandrakala-vatamsam*
*Bhakti-pradanaya kripa-vatheernam*
*Tam somanatham sharanam prapadye*

He, who has compassionately incarnated
In the sacred and delightful land of Saurashtra
He, who is resplendently luminous
Who dons the crescent of the moon
Who has come to bestow devotion and mercy
In that Somnath, I seek sanctuary.

Somaraj, also known as Chandra, was the radiant Moon God, illuminating the darkest of nights with his luminous presence. He was a renowned young deity, celebrated for his unmatched brilliance. His effulgent aura seemed to radiate from within, accentuating the contours of his chiselled features. This soft and warm light lent him an otherworldly charm, symbolizing a guiding light in the celestial and earthly realms alike.

Somaraj had twenty-seven wives, all of whom were daughters of Daksha Prajapati, Brahma's son. When giving his daughters' hands in marriage to Somaraj, Daksha Prajapati extracted a promise from him that he would not show any favouritism, and would treat all of his daughters with equal and unvarying love. He fervently wished that they would live together in peace, sharing the tapestry of their joys and sorrows as they had done thus far. This condition underscored Daksha's foresight in ensuring that their relationship would be rooted in equality and harmony, where each daughter could experience the richness of life's joys, and navigate its challenges with shared love and support.

The day of the wedding dawned – opulent, joyous, a kaleidoscope of colours. The daughters of Daksha were adorned in rich fabrics embroidered with intricate patterns, complemented by gorgeous jewellery set with the most precious of stones, each a reflection of the wearer's happiness. Somaraj too was bedecked in jewels, but the filigreed stones easily paled in comparison to his innate lustre.

As the priests intoned sacred verses of *shlokas* and scrupulously performed the rituals binding Somaraj and his wives in holy matrimony, the rhythmic beats of traditional music intertwined with joyous laughter formed the perfect symphony of celebration. On their marriage to Somaraj, the twenty-seven daughters of Daksha Prajapati began to glow brightly, much like their husband!

Daksha Prajapati's daughters were women of unparalleled beauty. Each exuded a regal grace, draped in resplendent attire that accentuated her exquisiteness, and each bearing subtle resemblances to her sisters. Their refined and delicate features perfectly mirrored and complemented Somaraj's own luminosity. Their matrimonial home seemed to shimmer with an ethereal charm, leaving an impression of a beautiful family united by both external grace and an inner regality.

All was not as it seemed.

Contrary to his promise, Somaraj found himself irresistibly drawn to his fourth wife, Rohini. Her shy and modest nature cast a captivating charm upon him, and her exquisite beauty compelled his attention. Despite his initial commitment to treat all his wives equally, the unique qualities possessed by Rohini stirred a particular fascination in Somaraj, ultimately influencing the dynamics of their shared matrimonial home and the sisterhood of Daksha's daughters.

Somaraj's every leisure moment became an exclusive retreat to Rohini, causing him to neglect his other wives. This triggered a tumult of emotions, stirring a mix of anger, envy and overwhelming sadness within the hearts of Rohini's sister-wives, who felt unfairly abandoned.

In the painful solitude of the time when Somaraj and Rohini were conspicuously absent, each of the neglected wives wrestled with a tangle of perplexing questions that tugged at the core of their feelings.

Kritika, the eldest and once the closest to Somaraj's heart, found herself questioning her own allure, pondering, 'Does he no longer see in me the grace that once captivated him? Is there a flaw in my beauty that now repels him?'

Chitra, once vivacious and spirited, grappled with a different set of insecurities. She wondered, 'Is it my vivacity that he finds tiresome?'

As for Bharani, the gentle and nurturing one, the contemplation went even deeper. She questioned, 'Have I, in my quest for gentleness, become a mere shadow in his eyes? Is he drawn to Rohini's boldness, and does he see my nurturing nature as a weakness?'

In their shared moments of confusion and vulnerability, the wives discussed their individual apprehensions. The ambience of the marital home the sisters shared became a commixture of melancholy and prying curiosity as they collectively speculated on the unsaid reasons behind Somaraj's disproportionate affections.

Anjali, the youngest and most sensitive among them, voiced her fears hesitantly, 'Do you think Rohini has cast some kind of spell on him? Is that why he seems bewitched and distant?'

Somaraj consistently sought opportunities to be in the company of Rohini, notwithstanding prior commitments to spend time with another sister. Despite reminders and entreaties, his attendance would often be begrudging, and his thoughts evidently preoccupied with Rohini. His departures, frequently premature, were justified by tenuous reasons, alluding to an urgent return to Rohini's side. So deeply immersed was he in his affection for her that he remained oblivious to the familial discord his actions engendered. Subsequently, he refrained from making any arrangements or pledges to partake in leisure activities with others unless Rohini's presence was assured.

On days when the sharp pangs of rejection cut through the hearts of his other wives with an unbearable intensity, their sense of loss was palpable. Vishakha, with tears welling in her eyes, whispered, 'Maybe he no longer sees us. Perhaps we have become mere ghosts in his world, overshadowed by the enchantment of Rohini.'

'Even when he is with us, he is not.'

As they entertained the notion that Rohini might have becharmed Somaraj, they exuded anguish and desperation. Deep within the recesses of their hearts, a seed of doubt sprouted, and the once-unshakable bond of sisterhood now faced the threat of unravelling in the face of heartache.

This pattern of differential treatment persisted, and as time wore on, the wives found it increasingly challenging to endure the repeated slights and indifference from their once-beloved husband. Wounded by the emotional toll of Somaraj's actions, they decided that they could no longer bear such a heart-wrenching situation. Driven by their shared pain, they resolved to seek solace by bringing their grievances to their father.

On a particularly pleasant day, the sisters, sans Rohini, gathered with their parents in the royal gardens to enjoy the lush greenery, vibrant blooms, chirping birds and buzzing bees, the place where many mirth-filled hours of their childhood had been spent. In stark contrast to the exuberant environment around them, they sat with shadowed faces and downcast eyes, barely enjoying the familiar atmosphere of their childhood home.

Daksha, seated regally in a carved wooden chair, observed his daughters with a furrowed brow, his gaze shifting between their faces. Watching with a curious concern the vulnerability etched on their faces, he waited for his beloved daughters to confide in him.

Unsure of how to broach such a delicate personal matter, they started, 'Father! You know that we have always loved and respected you. Your wish was always our command and we have never crossed you or done anything to upset you or sully your illustrious name.' The daughters, their eyes glistening with unshed tears, revealed the anguish of feeling unloved and neglected by Somaraj.

'When you fixed our marriage with the dynamic and ever-radiant Somaraj, we happily obliged. Why, we were even elated that all us sisters would not be separated even after our marriage. We looked forward to starting this new chapter of our lives together. The loving and caring father that you are, always thinking of the well-being of his daughters, you ensured that there would never be any dearth for us for anything that we could ever want or need. Before marrying us off to the man who is now our husband, you extracted a promise from him. You ensured that he would treat us all the same, equally, with love and respect.'

They paused, unsure how to proceed further to the crux of the issue at hand. Trying to mask his rising concern and fearing the worst, Daksha Prajapati looked on at his beloved daughters, waiting patiently, unsure of where exactly this conversation was headed.

'But alas, dear Father, this is not the case. 'Our married life is not as blissful as you had wished it to be. It is not filled with joy or happiness. In fact, as the days have gone by, we are feeling more and more alienated in our own matrimonial home.'

Daksha Prajapati, who loved his daughters more than anything in the world, looked from one beautiful face creased with pain to another. 'What is the matter, my lovely daughters?' he said. 'What is bothering you? Tell me at once and I will ensure that it will be taken care of!'

'Oh, Father!' his daughters cried. 'We are feeling unloved because that is precisely how we are being treated by our dear husband Somaraj. He has slowly begun to favour our dear sister Rohini over all of us. This would not have been an issue in itself, as it is natural for every person to have a favourite, and we were happy for her, but the situation has now become unbearable.

'What started out as one wife being more beloved than the others has now turned into neglect and avoidance of the others. Our husband does not see us anymore. He does not visit us; he does not spend time with any of us. He does not even stop to look at us and ask us if we are happy and well. He spends all his time with Rohini. And when he is not with Rohini, he pines for her. If we try to talk to him and reason with him, he only gets angry with us.

'Tell us, dear Father, how are we expected to fulfil our marital duties and live happily married lives if our husband does not visit us, and we do not even occupy a small place in his mind and heart? He has blatantly ignored and violated the promise he made to you before marrying us as he clearly would like to spend all his time with Rohini alone.

'Are we lacking in something, Father? Is something so horribly wrong with us that our husband does not even wish to see us?'

The daughters' pleas rang through the well-tended floral thickets, their voices of collective distress rising above the cacophony of the birds as they questioned their worth.

Daksha Prajapati could not bear to see the tears of anguish and pain in his daughters' eyes. The girls that he had so lovingly brought up, without even a silhouette of pain or discomfort, now stood before him, baring their deepest sorrows to him. He took it upon himself to have a word with Somaraj and try to implant some sense of responsibility in him.

Daksha strode into his daughters' palatial marital home with a sense of purpose. On seeing him, Somaraj welcomed him as one must a father-in-law. 'Sire! I am so happy that you have come to visit the home of your daughters. You will be happy to see that your precious darlings are being tended to with the utmost love and care, in a manner fit for the greatest of queens! Please, take a seat. I shall summon refreshments to make our time together even more enjoyable.' He bowed reverentially.

Daksha Prajapati barely registered his son-in-law's warm welcome, so lost was he in the labyrinth of his thoughts. His focus was singular, dedicated to finding the most delicate and effective approach to address the pressing matter at hand.

As he navigated the complex currents of his mind, Daksha grappled with the challenge of safeguarding his daughters' well-being without inadvertently stoking the flames of discord. He sought a path that would bring relief to his precious darlings without inciting further discomfort in their lives.

Amid these internal deliberations, Daksha Prajapati recognized that a direct approach might be the best recourse. The urgency of the situation demanded forthrightness. His daughters' happiness hung in the balance, and he was determined to find a way to improve their lives without exacerbating the fragile situation.

'Somaraj, beloved son-in-law, I have come to reason with you and shed light on the error in your ways. Equal affection for all my daughters was a precondition to your marriage to them. Failing in this will breed ill-will and animosity among your wives, disrupting the peace within your household. Such behaviour will only lead to pain.'

Somaraj, taken aback by Daksha Prajapati's unexpected outburst, responded defensively, 'Father-in-law, what do you mean? I respect all your daughters equally. Since their arrival, my house has been filled with love and laughter. These are the most blissful of times!'

Daksha realized Somaraj was oblivious to the pain his actions caused his other wives. Slowly, he asked, 'Tell me, Somaraj, do you not favour one daughter over the others? Do you not have a favourite wife whom you prefer to spend all your time with?'

Somaraj, smiling sheepishly, insisted, 'No, Father-in-law! I love all my wives,' but his conviction wavered.

Daksha pressed on, 'Come on, Son-in-law. I know Rohini is your favoured one.'

Somaraj's face brightened at the mention of Rohini, but Daksha continued, 'I am thankful my daughter has a loving husband, but I have twenty-six other daughters married to you. I cannot fail in my duty towards them, and neither should you.'

Somaraj looked at him questioningly. 'What is the matter, Father-in-law? Are my wives facing difficulties? This has not been brought to my notice. Tell me, and it will be taken care of.'

Daksha replied, 'Somaraj, openly favouring one wife causes jealousy and anger. While you spend time with Rohini, you are unjust to my other daughters. Your neglect has hurt them deeply, and if not rectified, it will sow discord in your family. You are youthful and have much to learn. Consider this your first and most important lesson on marital life.'

Somaraj attempted to speak, 'But—'

Daksha continued sternly without pausing to hear Somaraj's response, 'Do not forget, Son-in-law, that you promised to treat them all equally with love, respect and care. I trust you will honour your words. This matter should not be discussed again. I expect you to mend your ways and ensure the happiness of all my daughters. If you fail in your duties, you shall have me to reckon with...' With those firm words, Daksha Prajapati left, leaving behind the weight of his expectations.

Satisfied with the course of the conversation, Daksha believed that the issue would be swiftly resolved. He had confidence in his son-in-law and assumed he would uphold his commitment to being a responsible and caring husband.

However, the next time Daksha's daughters visited, he could not help but notice the despondency etched in their faces. Their eyes, once vibrant, now appeared sunken, and their lackadaisical attire signalled a departure from their usual elegance.

Surprised and concerned, Daksha remarked, 'My darling daughters, what is the matter? Why are you dressed so?'

Their response was laden with bitterness. 'What is the point of dressing up when even our husband does not see us?'

Puzzled, Daksha enquired, 'What do you mean?'

Their collective retort painted a grim picture. 'Did you speak to our husband? Or should we say Rohini's husband? Somaraj does not even remember us anymore. We do not see him for days. He spends all his time with Rohini. He does not even acknowledge us. In his eyes, he has only one wife. We are just the sisters of Rohini. He has not kept his promise to you, Father. We feel like outsiders in our own home.' Their words were laced with anguish.

Daksha could not bear to witness their agony. He had nurtured them with love and affection, envisioning a future of happiness, not one tarnished by continual disregard from their husband.

He barged into Somaraj's palace, his face red with anger. Somaraj rose to greet his father-in-law, but Daksha did not wait to complete the niceties.

'How dare you treat my daughters like this!' he roared, his voice filled with righteous anger. Despite Somaraj's attempts to speak, Daksha continued, expressing acute disappointment in his son-in-law. He did not give Somaraj a chance to defend himself. 'You shall pay for your sins, O son-in-law. You have broken your promise. Clearly, you are not a man of your word.'

Daksha's accusatory tone bore the burden of his daughters' suffering. 'Have you even looked at any of your wives' faces, anyone except Rohini? Their radiance has faded because of you. You ignore them, dismiss them, and, worst of all, fail to be a loving husband to them.'

Somaraj, guilt-ridden and aware of the truth in Daksha's words, could not meet his father-in-law's gaze.

Daksha's anger remained unabated, and he cursed Somaraj with a vehement proclamation. 'May your powers decline with every passing day. May you lay wasted and fall prey to a rotting disease as a result of your actions!' With these words, Daksha Prajapati stormed away, leaving Somaraj to contemplate the consequences of his choices.

Thereafter, Somaraj's luminous radiance began to wane, and he soon appeared weak and sickly with an unprecedented disease.

Rohini, immersed in the bliss of her love for Somaraj, had remained oblivious to the emotional turmoil brewing among her sisters. She had failed to notice the changes in their demeanour and the discontent that had settled on their faces. It was not until her father's curse began to show its effect that she became mindful of the unrest. Realizing the gravity of the situation, she took it upon herself to convince her resentful sisters to stand by their ailing husband.

'It is your *dharma*,' she counselled them.

'Why must we always be burdened with his care? It is not our duty to tend to him every time he falters.'

'Exactly! Rohini, you were always his favourite. He should rely on you for comfort, not us.'

'But he is your husband too! We have a duty to support him in his time of need.' Rohini struggled to reason with her sisters as she began to realize just how much they had been tormented.

'Well, he never seemed to care much for us, did he?'

'That is not fair! He may have his preferences, but that does not absolve us of our responsibilities,' Rohini protested.

'What responsibilities?' the sisters continued. 'He has never once acknowledged our efforts.'

'Regardless of his affections, we have a duty to him, whether he appreciates it or not,' Rohini repeated, unable to defend her and Somaraj's action any other way.

Despite her efforts and appeals to their sense of duty, her advice fell on deaf ears. The sisters remained unmoved by the deterioration of Somaraj's once-lustrous visage, and Rohini found herself helpless in the face of their indifference.

After some time passed and the sisters had the opportunity to deliberate, they reluctantly resolved to visit their husband, their footsteps heavy with trepidation as they approached his bedside. There, they were met with a heart-wrenching sight – a once-vibrant and commanding figure was now reduced to a frail and deteriorating state. Shock and desolation gripped their hearts as they beheld the extent of his decline.

'Oh no... This can't be...'

'He looks so weak... How did it come to this?'

'He looks almost unrecognizable, lacklustre...'

The sister-wives turned to each other, their faces etched with sorrow and regret. They knew they had never harboured intentions to inflict such grievous harm upon their husband; their only desire was to be treated with fairness and equity in return for their love and care. Yet, as they stood there, confronted with the stark reality of his suffering, a deep sense of guilt gnawed at their souls.

'We must do something. We cannot just stand by and watch our husband waste away.'

'But who can help us?'

After some thought and deliberation, they resolved to seek aid from the *devas*, who could be aware of a solution to the ailments of Somaraj, a *deva* himself. For they understood that they could no longer bear to witness their beloved husband's pain, and they were determined to set things right, no matter the cost.

The *devas*, distressed by Somaraj's condition, approached Lord Brahma. 'Somaraj has been cursed by Daksha Prajapati, and he has become weak and fragile. Please help him!' they pleaded, their pellucid faces creased with concern for the Lord of the Moon.

Brahma, seated atop a magnificent white lotus, responded with a mix of joy and contempt. 'Somaraj deserves it!' he scoffed, questioning the *devas* about Somaraj's past indiscretions. 'Your concern for him is highly misplaced.' Brahma's disdainful tone left the *devas* with a stark reminder of the consequences of Somaraj's carelessness.

Rishi Brihaspati was the chief priest of the *devas* residing in *Indra loka*, the heavenly abode of the *devas*. His wife, Tara, a priestess in her own right, assisted him in performing the holy rituals for the *devas*. Always dressed in ivory-white in contrast to the other flamboyant residents of *Indra loka*, Tara did not require any adornments to look as charming as the other maidens of the locale. Her beauty was not merely skin-deep; it was the embodiment of her character, grace and a timeless allure matched only by her exhaustive knowledge of the holy scriptures, rituals and spiritual practices.

Brihaspati diligently performed the duties arising from his post, and was unable to optimally navigate the complexities of his austere duties and marital obligations. Tara often found herself to be lonely and without companionship for days on end when her husband was either lost in thought on how to aid the *devas* in their latest conquests, or immersed in *yagnas* and other rituals that were pivotal to the residents of *Indra loka* for their continued health, wealth and vigour.

Somaraj, who came to visit *Indra loka,* laid his eyes on Tara and instantly fell in love with her. Tara too, feeling trapped in what she felt was a loveless marriage to Brihaspati, became equally enamoured with the radiant Somaraj. She willingly chose to leave *Indra loka* and join Somaraj in the skies.

The revelation of Tara's departure triggered a storm of emotions within Brihaspati. How could anyone have the courage to abduct the wife of the chief priest of *Indra loka*? Feeling wronged and betrayed, a livid Brihaspati stormed into Indra's court and demanded an immediate audience with the king of the *devas*.

On hearing Brihaspati's hurried narration of the unfortunate abduction of his beloved wife, the *devas* gathered in the opulent hall mirrored his fury, appalled by the embarrassment Somaraj's actions had inflicted upon their esteemed chief priest. Brihaspati's warning to the *devas* reverberated through the majestic audience gathered at Indra's palace, 'Bring my wife back to me or I will not preside over any of your *yagnas* or perform any of your rituals.' The gravity of his ultimatum hung in the air, propelling the *devas* to rectify the situation.

At this, Indra and the other *devas* rallied their troops and stormed off to Somaraj's abode. First, they attempted to reason with him.

'Allow Tara to return to her husband,' they implored, their voices echoing their concern for the sanctity of Tara's marriage to Brihaspati.

'She is a married woman. You cannot keep her with you,' they urged, emphasizing the violation of the norms that Somaraj's actions represented. The tension in the hall escalated as the *devas* sought to persuade Somaraj to rectify the transgression.

'You are living in sin, but you can rectify the situation and claim responsibility for your actions,' they cajoled, desperately appealing to his sense of morality, but Somaraj remained unmoved in the face of their appeals.

Enraged, the *devas* attacked Somaraj in an attempt to bring Tara back to *Indra loka*, but Somaraj cleverly hid among the *daityas* and fought them effortlessly, without any forethought about how his actions could backfire.

Frustrated and unable to subdue Somaraj, the *devas* approached Lord Brahma and Maharishi Atri. The maharishi was Somaraj's father and Lord Brahma his grandfather, and both of them were extremely disappointed by Somaraj's behaviour and strongly condemned his actions. After much debate and persuasion, under the weight of the familial and hierarchical authority of his antecedents, Somaraj assented to Tara's return to Brihaspati.

Tara, realizing that she and Somaraj could never be together and that there was no other recourse, returned to *Indra loka* and her husband. While she carried on as though everything was as before, Brihaspati, astute and observant, noticed a subtle transformation in Tara. Now with child, Tara carried within her the consequences of a truth that would unravel the foundation of their once-sacred union.

Brihaspati, gripped by a mixture of emotions ranging from anxiety to a sense of betrayal, confronted his wife. 'Whose child are you carrying?' he enquired.

Tara, calm but burdened by the truth, did not respond immediately.

'Whose child are you carrying?' he repeated impatiently, on the precipice of anger and consternation, dreading the revelation that loomed over the couple struggling to hold on to what was left of their relationship.

Meeting her husband's gaze with a calm resolve, Tara finally responded, 'It is Somaraj's child.'

Lord Brahma concluded his narration solemnly, 'I had to intervene between Somaraj and Brihaspati once again to ensure that there would not be any further altercation regarding Tara's child.' The tension in the gathering of the *devas* was unimaginable as they were reminded of the events past.

After a thoughtful pause, Lord Brahma continued to address the concerned *devas*. 'Somaraj's actions were wrong and unfair to his other wives. While this angers me as well, the debilitation of Somaraj, this enfeebling, cannot go on for much longer. The world needs Chandra.'

With immaculate wisdom, Lord Brahma unveiled the key to the intricate problem. 'There is a way for him to repent his wrongdoings. He must chant the *Mahamrutyunjaya Mantra* at the holy ground of Prabhas Patan, and a solution will present itself,' he declared, outlining the path to redemption for Somaraj.

Somaraj, who had had some time to contemplate his actions, upon receiving this guidance, wasted no time. Driven by a deep sense of fidelity and repentance, he embarked on a journey to the sacred site. There, amid the sanctity of Prabhas Patan, Somaraj began the arduous task of chanting the powerful mantra, seeking forgiveness for his transgressions.

Time seemed to stretch into eternity as Somaraj immersed himself in the consecrated practices. Pleased with the sincerity of his penance, Lord Shiva, in His beatific glory, manifested before him. 'I am pleased with your devout penance,' He said, acknowledging the transformation in Somaraj's heart. 'Ask me for anything you want, and it shall be granted.'

Without hesitation, a humbled Somaraj lamented before the overarching presence. 'O Mahadeva! I am so blessed to see You in all Your glory. I have wronged my wives by neglecting them, and by the curse of their father, Daksha Prajapati, I am paying the ultimate price for my cruel actions. My power and health have been deteriorating with every passing day. I have now understood the error of my ways. Please rid me of this curse, O Lord,' he pleaded.

In a moment of compassion, Mahadeva gazed upon Somaraj with benevolent eyes and spoke, 'Somaraj, you are aware, just as well as anyone, that once a curse has been spoken, it cannot be revoked. However, I discern that you have grasped the lessons of your actions. I shall modify your curse. Your powers will surge during *shukla paksha,* the waxing lunar cycle, for fifteen days, only to diminish during *krishna paksha*, the waning phase, for the next fifteen days. On full moon days, you shall grace the world with your mesmerizing radiance, while on new moon days, you will fade away. This adjustment will fulfil Daksha Prajapati's curse while allowing a concordant balance with your lunar duties that guide the world.'

Somaraj was crestfallen that he was unable to rid himself of the curse completely.

Observing his state, Mahadeva, in His infinite benevolence, spoke words of reassurance. 'Do not look so dejected, Soma. You will retain all your powers,' He consoled Somaraj, bestowing a glimmer of hope unto his troubled heart.

'While the crescent moon will be a reminder of your curse, it will ensure that you do not return to your old ways, and serve as a cautionary tale for others too.' Mahadeva continued, outlining the heavenly symbol that would bear witness to Somaraj's journey to redemption.

In a sincere gesture of solidarity, Mahadeva made a solemn commitment, cementing the bond between deity and devotee. 'I will wear the crescent moon in my hair to show devotees how dear you are to me. And thus, you will always be near me. From now on, I will also be known as Someshwar.'

*Thus, Lord Shiva came to be known by the names of* Someshwar and Chandrashekhar or 'the one with the moon mounted on his head'. Once a week, Somvar or Monday is dedicated to the moon.

Somaraj's twenty-seven wives are considered to be constellations that surround the moon's orbit today. The names of his wives are Kritika, Rohini, Mrigashirsha, Ardra, Punarvasu, Purbabhadrapada, Pushya, Alesha, Magha, Svati, Chitra, Purvaphalguni, Hasta, Radha, Vishakha, Anuradha, Jyeshta, Mula, Purbashadha, Uttarashara, Sravana, Uttaraphalguni, Satabhisha, Uttarabhadrapada, Revati, Ashwini and Bharani.

The place where the Someshwar (also referred to as Somnath) *jyotirlinga* has been installed has been referred to as *Prabhas Kshetra* in the *Purana*s. This is a result of Mahadeva proclaiming to Somaraj, 'Henceforth, this land shall be named after your regained *prabhas*, your lustre.'

The correlation between the Somnath *jyotirlinga* and the Vedas, as described in the *Shiva Purana*, adds a profound layer to the significance of this sacred site. The establishment of the *jyotirlinga* is intricately aligned with the four Vedas – *Rig*, *Yajur*, *Sama* and *Atharva* – correlating with the dawn, noon, dusk and night of a day.

Parvati had once asked Mahadeva why the Somnath *jyotirlinga* is referred to by so many names. In response to her query, He told her that just as Brahma nears the end of every *kalpa* and the new Brahma takes his place, in the same manner, in every *kalpa*, the Someshwar *jyotirlinga* acquires and is referred to by a different name. In some of the previous *kalpa*s, Somnath was referred to as Mrityunjay, Kalagnirudra, Amritesh and Prannath, among other names. Mahadeva went on to tell her that the Someshwar *jyotirlinga* is eternal in nature.

In *Kali yuga*, during which there is an exponential increase in the sins committed by living beings, Mahadeva instructed His son Ganesha to never leave the side of the Someshwar *jyotirlinga*, thus always protecting it and ensuring that this *jyotirlinga* is easily accessible to all of Mahadeva's ardent devotees. 'Of all the *linga*s present on earth,' Mahadeva said, 'Somnath is especially dear to me!'

The famous Somnath Temple is located in Saurashtra, Gujarat.

Most dear to Lord Shiva, Somnath is the first of the twelve *jyotirlingas*.

# MALLIKARJUNA
## Sibling Rivalry and a Mother's Love

*Shri-shaila-shringe vibhudati-sange*
*Tula-dritunge-pi muda vasantam*
*Tamarjunam mallika-purvamenam*
*Namami samsara-samudra-setum*

He, who resides on the peak of Srisailam
Higher than the highest precursor of mountains
Where all the gods gather
He, who is as a bridge across the Ocean of Life
To the sole god called Mallikarjuna
I bow.

Mahadeva's elder son Kartikeya was brave and determined, while Ganesha, His younger son, was acclaimed for his acute knowledge and wittiness.

Kartikeya was distinguished in *swarga loka* for his valour, strength and strategies employed in wars against the *asuras*. This is how he came to be known as the God of War. He is also affectionately called Kumara, Muruga and Skanda by his devotees.

Kartikeya, always seen adorned with ornaments, exudes a radiant aura that symbolizes his legendary prowess. His countenance reflects a perfect blend of grace and determination, capturing the essence of a warrior god.

In each of his four right arms, Kartikeya wields a formidable array of weapons, showcasing his martial supremacy. The diamond sword in one hand signifies his sharp intellect and decisiveness in battle. The plough represents his role in cultivating virtue, while the mace symbolizes his strength. A goad serves as a tool for guiding devotees along the righteous path. In his four left arms, he brandishes a *trishul*, a shield, a noose and an arrow, each representing varied aspects of authoritative power and protection.

Perched majestically beside Kartikeya is his chosen *vahana*, the beautiful peacock named Paravani. The peacock is not merely a mode of transportation but also a symbol of beauty, resilience, and victory over vanity.

Ganesha is adorned by a large elephant head, complemented by ears mirroring the grandeur of his visage. His thick trunk gracefully curves to one side, delicately cradling a *modak* – a confection. In his primary right hand, Ganesha wields a broken tusk, earning him the name '*Ekdanta*' or single-tusked, a poignant symbol of sacrifice and the willingness to surmount obstacles for the greater good. The other deft hands of Ganesha hold a noose and a goad, symbolizing control over desires and gentle guidance along the righteous path. At his side, a small mouse, Mooshika, accompanies him as a loyal *vahana*, underscoring humility and the recognition of wisdom.

The two brothers, Kartikeya and Ganesha, with their unique attributes and distinct personalities, brought both valour and wisdom to the heavenly abode they shared with their parents. Ganesha's arrival completed the family and filled the seraphic household with laughter and joy. It seemed that he was the favoured one of Mahadeva, who had Himself breathed life into his body.

The brothers grew up together, experiencing the usual dynamics of sibling relationships – love, fights, joy, jealousy, pranks and competitions – all under the loving and watchful eyes of their parents, Mahadeva and Parvati.

What began as innocent childhood competition between the brothers gradually evolved into a deep-seated and intense sibling rivalry over the years. Their ongoing feud escalated to a point where they reached a deadlock. Their competition extended from trivial matters to ultimately centring around marriage, sparking a quarrel only siblings could engage in.

'I am the elder one, and I have vanquished many *asuras*. It is but logical for me to be the first to get married!' Kartikeya expressed, rolling his eyes at his younger brother.

Ganesha, with steadfast determination, defied his brother's logic. 'My being younger than you cannot be the sole reason for me to follow in your footsteps. I refuse to be second to you in this regard.'

Mahadeva and Parvati, witnessing the escalating conflict between their sons, observed as it transformed into a heated argument. The brothers, fuelled by anger, began to engage in disputes whenever they were in each other's presence. Their irritated whispers, and unreasonable statements and declarations disrupted the serene atmosphere of snow-clad Kailasha, leaving their parents concerned about the resolution of this familial discord.

Mahadeva and Parvati decided to intervene. After thoughtful deliberation, they devised a unique method to settle the matter. Seated on a snow bench covered with the skin of a tiger for warmth, they awaited the arrival of Kartikeya and Ganesha, whom they had summoned.

As the brothers approached, both bowed respectfully to their parents, standing deliberately apart, refusing to acknowledge each other's presence.

Parvati, with a radiant smile, addressed her sons, 'My darling sons! Mahadeva and I have been silent witnesses to your quarrels and subsequent reconciliations over the years, and never interfered. However, this time, unlike ever before, neither of you seems willing to back down, see reason, or extend the courtesy of coming to an agreement. It has now reached a stage where even we find it difficult to ignore.'

The sons sighed in derision, their expressions reflecting annoyance with each other, still avoiding eye contact to emphasize their mutual discontent.

Despite the strained atmosphere, Parvati spoke with maternal firmness: 'As is the usual way for siblings, we patiently waited for many a day for the two of you to find a way to resolve your disagreement, as you always have done in the past. But this can go on no longer.

'Taking matters into our own hands, we have decided that it is time for us to help resolve this matter. We love you both equally and adore you more than life itself, hence we have put much thought into how to tackle this situation without further alienating either of you from the other.'

She paused, glancing at her husband, expecting His input on the matter.

Taking the cue, Mahadeva continued, 'Having listened to both of you, we understand that it is important for the both of you to get married, and get married first, that is, before the other.'

'I. . .'

'Yes. . .'

The two boys nodded vigorously and were about to speak, but Parvati interrupted them. 'We have devised a test of your abilities, wisdom and knowledge. Whoever can persevere and emerge with a satisfactory result will be the first to get married.'

Kartikeya and Ganesha directed their attention towards their parents, their countenances displaying a subtle curiosity. Uncertain whether their parents' intentions were earnest or not, they perceived their request as a novel approach to addressing the issue at hand. Together, they inquired, 'What course of action do you propose, dear parents?'

'Whichever one of you travels around the world three times first will be the first to get married,' Parvati declared, observing her sons' expressions closely.

The two boys were stumped! What sort of test was this? How would this determine who would be fit to get married first? So many questions lingered, but neither of them dared to question their parents and risk further complications or disappointment.

Kartikeya, ever eager and poised for action, signalled to Paravani that he was setting off on the mission outlined by his parents. A seasoned warrior, always prepared for any challenge that came his way, he mounted the majestic blue-green peacock and urged her to soar at breakneck speed around the world. The fluttering of Paravani's wings marked the commencement of the race.

Meanwhile, Ganesha stood contemplatively, his thoughtful gaze fixed upon his parents. The weight of the challenge slowly unfolded before him, and he began to grasp the mammoth nature of the task set by Mahadeva and Parvati.

In a tableau of parental love, Mahadeva and Parvati sat in silence, keenly observing the distinct approaches of their two sons. The duo witnessed the unfolding drama with a tranquil demeanour.

To Kartikeya's surprise, he swiftly completed one round around the world, only to find Ganesha standing still. Amused by the thought of Mooshika attempting a leisurely circumnavigation, Kartikeya burst into laughter, confident that victory was within his grasp.

As he neared the completion of his second round, urgency and exhilaration engulfed him with an all-too-familiar feeling of victory being just ahead of his reach.

Mahadeva, intrigued by the events, calmly addressed Ganesha, His curiosity evident, 'My dear son, what occupies your thoughts? Despite the prolonged debates with your brother, now that it is time to prove yourself, you show no inclination to compete against him.'

Ganesha, as if awakened from a ruminative reverie, gazed at his father. Without uttering a word, he silently beckoned Mooshika, who stood ready for his summons. Mounting his *vahana* with deliberate calmness, he directed the small mouse to circle the snow bench on which his parents were seated.

Parvati observed her son's actions with a questioning look, seeking an understanding of his strategy. Meanwhile, Mahadeva, with insight, smiled serenely, recognizing the profundity of Ganesha's intentions.

Ganesha completed three rounds around his parents, bowing in reverence before them.

In that moment, Kartikeya returned, having completed his third round around the world. Seeing Ganesha still near his parents, he laughed triumphantly and declared, 'I have won!'

However, Ganesha calmly addressed his parents: 'You are my world. My world is where you both reside. By circumnavigating you three times, I have, in essence, encircled the entire world.'

Kartikeya stood in stunned silence, his features a canvas of conflicting emotions. After a moment of speechlessness, he scoffed in disbelief, 'This is unacceptable. Ganesha did not even leave Kailasha!' He threw a challenging glance at his parents, questioning the fairness of the outcome.

Mahadeva and Parvati exchanged a knowing look, observing their sons – Ganesha, composed, and Kartikeya, still catching his breath. Mahadeva, the embodiment of wisdom, finally spoke, addressing His sons, 'My illustrious children, you each possess your unique strengths and purposes in this Universe – one, fierce and ever-ready for battle, the other, calm, insightful and wise in the ways of life and relationships.'

Ganesha remained rooted, awaiting the final decision, while Kartikeya shifted restlessly, a growing sense of loss apparent in his demeanour. Mahadeva continued, 'Kartikeya, my valiant child, undefeated in battles, your strength is admirable. However, maturity comes with time, and you still have much to learn before taking on the responsibilities that marriage entails.'

Turning to Ganesha, Mahadeva acknowledged, 'Ganesha, you took your time to understand the true meaning of our challenge. Patiently, you navigated it, placing your love and respect for us above all else.'

With a decisive declaration, Mahadeva announced, 'Ganesha will be the one to get married first!'

Ganesha, though joyous at having bested his brother, remained grounded and bowed to his parents reverentially. On the other hand, Kartikeya, wrestling with the unexpected turn of events, slumped away without a second glance, unable to process the startling outcome.

Parvati smiled endearingly at Ganesha, her heart brimming with pride at his love and ardour for his parents, before a wave of worry darkened her ethereal features as she watched Kartikeya walk away, his head steeped in defeat.

Throughout this epic battle of valour and wits, Narada Muni, known for his eternal travels, took a brief pause to savour the spectacle of sibling rivalry unfolding before him. Such disagreements of an extreme magnitude, which may have far-reaching impact, were not an everyday occurrence even in the vast expanse of the Universe.

Hidden amid the clouds, Narada Muni observed the events taking place below as Mahadeva declared Ganesha the victor. The sage, with his unique ability to transcend spheres of reality and existence, witnessed the intricate dynamics of this immortal family.

Meanwhile, Kartikeya, nursing the wounds of defeat and a touch of soreness, distanced himself from the familial gathering. Seated afar, he struggled to contemplate the nuances of the challenge and its meaningful implications.

Seizing the chance to stir up some chaos, Narada Muni, his eyes gleaming mischievously, descended from the wispy clouds. Slowly making his way towards Kartikeya, the sage observed the brooding and dejected warrior. Recognizing a holy presence before him, Kartikeya hastily rose and bowed before the sage, his thoughts still entangled in the recent turn of events.

'Narayana! Narayana!' Narada Muni greeted, bestowing a blessing upon Kartikeya as he settled down beside him. The learned seer, notorious for his penchant for mischief and wisdom, prepared to engage Kartikeya in a conversation.

'What is bothering you, my child?' Narada Muni enquired, his tone carrying a sense of genuine concern, as if the brotherly challenge had not just unfolded before his eyes. Kartikeya, still nursing the wounds of his recent trouncing, averted his gaze, reluctant to confide in the sage. After some gentle prodding from Narada, Kartikeya hesitantly began recounting the events past, unaware that the sage was already well-acquainted with the ongoings.

Upon hearing the warrior god's sombre soliloquy, Narada Muni's brow furrowed as he feigned cogitation. Slowly, he responded, 'It appears to me that your parents perceive Ganesha to be the more mature sibling, despite his younger age and fewer accolades to his name.'

Kartikeya, yearning to find affirmation for his thoughts, nodded in concurrence. However, coming up short in any trial or tribulation is not taken lightly by a warrior, and so, the burden of shame lingered evidently on his dauntless features.

'I have suffered humiliation at the hands of my younger brother,' Kartikeya lamented. 'I am the God of War, facing challenges daily, and yet, I lost such an easy contest to him. What will the other *devas* think?' He looked entreatingly at Narada, seeking solace or guidance from the sage.

Narada Muni, relishing the opportunity to impart his wisdom, took his time to expel some compassion and offer up a remedy. 'If only there was something you could do to convince your parents of your maturity. You are more than just battle strategies and war cries...' he mused, purposefully leaving the statement open-ended to gauge Kartikeya's response.

Kartikeya took the bait just as expected, responding, 'Tell me, Narada Muni, the most revered one. Tell me what I can do to prove myself to my parents. It is as though my father does not believe in my prowess outside of the battlefield, and my mother's silence shows that she agrees with Him.' The warrior god's determination to prove himself beyond the confines of war was indisputable.

Sage Narada fixed his erudite gaze on Kartikeya and said, 'My valiant child, battles and victories are not the only measures of maturity. There exists a zone beyond the clangour of war cries, where the depth of your character can shine. Why not consider penance? A display of strength not only in the battlefield but within yourself, showcasing to your parents the multifarious layers of your wisdom and maturity. By doing so, who knows, you may even set out on a path of self-examination and discern dimensions of yourself that will only enhance your self-awareness, and in turn, your martial acumen.'

Kartikeya, his curiosity piqued and fortitude ablaze, queried, 'Penance, you say? A chance to reveal my strength beyond the battlefield intrigues me. I shall undertake this journey, for the well-being you speak of and to prove to my parents that my maturity extends beyond battle.'

With a nod of approval from Narada, Kartikeya embarked on his journey to the Kraunch Mountain. As he left, Narada's words lingered: 'May your penance unfold the untold facets of your being, my courageous child.'

Under the guidance of Narada Muni, Kartikeya enthusiastically embraced the idea of undertaking penance on Mount Kraunch. After completing the necessary formalities with his parents, he set off for the mountain to commence his spiritual practice. As Kartikeya immersed himself in deep meditation on

Mount Kraunch, his absence began to deeply affect his parents in Kailasha, particularly causing Parvati to feel increasingly distressed and lonely.

In Kailasha, the maternal yearning silently burgeoned within Parvati. Bereft of Kartikeya's vibrant companionship, the creases of worry etched upon her brow only deepened, mirroring the motherly apprehension that enveloped her soul.

One day, unable to contain her anxiety any longer, Parvati approached Mahadeva. With a heavy heart, she spoke, 'My Lord, a disquietude grips me. Kartikeya's absence weighs heavily on my soul. Have our decisions been too rigid, and has my dearth of support impacted him more deeply than we comprehend?'

Mahadeva placed a reassuring hand on Parvati's shoulder. 'Precious Parvati, the path of penance is a journey each soul must undertake to discover its depths. Kartikeya's prowess transcends mere battlefield valour. However, he must navigate this path of self-discovery independently. His penance is a testament to his multifaceted maturity, a journey he willingly chose. Let us trust in his resilience and allow him to unravel the layers of his being.'

Parvati, momentarily comforted by Mahadeva's wisdom, nodded timidly. Together, they decided to watch over Kartikeya's penance, with Mahadeva's unyielding faith in His son and Parvati's motherly concern for his well-being.

Mahadeva looked lovingly at His consort and said 'O Parvati, do not worry. Our son has gone to conduct deep penance. We must be happy for him and await its successful completion. He shall return soon. Please do not look so sad. I cannot bear to see you this way.'

As Kartikeya immersed himself in penance on the solitary slopes of Mount Kraunch, the heaviness of Parvati's heart continued to weigh her down. Unable to find succour, Parvati's worry continued to deepen despite Mahadeva's counsel.

Observing His beloved consort's distress, Mahadeva decided to intercede. He called upon a group of *devas* and entrusted them with a delicate task – to persuade Kartikeya to return to Mount Kailasha.

The emissaries approached the place where Kartikeya was absorbed in his penance.

'Great Lord Kartikeya,' spoke one of the *devas*, 'we come as messengers from Kailasha, carrying the heartfelt concerns of your parents. The air in your absence is heavy with Parvati's sorrow, and Mahadeva Himself yearns for your return to the warm embrace of your family.'

Kartikeya, seated in deep meditation, opened his eyes to acknowledge the tense visitors. His countenance, marked by the intensity of his penance, revealed a resolute spirit and a tinge of melancholy. The *devas* continued, expressing the longing that permeated the sacred abode, the yearning for the return of the valiant son who had embarked on a spiritual quest.

With a voice that diffused both determination and sorrow, Kartikeya replied, 'Revered *devas*, I appreciate the love and concern that fills your words. However, my path of penance is guided by a higher purpose, and I am bound by a commitment to seek spiritual enlightenment. Assure my parents that I am well and under the benevolent gaze of the forces guiding my journey.'

The *devas*, understanding the gravity of the warrior's chosen path, bowed respectfully before retreating, carrying his message back to the sacred terrain of Kailasha.

Based on the narration of the proceedings on Mount Kraunch by the *devas*, Mahadeva and Parvati deliberated on the best course of action. A longing to be in their beloved son's presence overcame them.

With a congruent understanding, Mahadeva and Parvati decided to embark on a journey to visit him at Mount Kraunch. The prospect of reuniting with Kartikeya filled their hearts with delight.

However, as the news of their impending visit reached Kartikeya's ears, he became determined that his penance should not be disturbed. The resolute warrior subtly moved his place of meditation three *yojanas* away from Mount Kraunch. The spiritual vibrations surrounding him remained undisturbed, creating a secluded haven where he could continue his expiation.

Unaware of their son's evasion, Mahadeva and Parvati set forth towards Mount Kraunch.

Upon reaching, the two were awestruck by the spiritual aura enveloping the region. The climate around Kartikeya, charged from his intense penance, now also had the love of his parents, seeking a way to reconnect with him, seeping in.

Mahadeva, the epitome of stoicism, admired the determination and commitment displayed by His son. The warrior god's pursuit of spiritual understanding, even at the cost of physical separation, was accordant with Mahadeva's own appreciation for the arduous journey of self-discovery.

Parvati, on the other hand, felt an overwhelming surge of maternal love. Her heart, brimming with fondness for Kartikeya, ached with the longing to be close to him. Despite the disappointment of not finding him at the originally chosen spot, her love for her son remained unaltered.

In a moment of thoughtful parental unity and as a regard for Kartikeya's journey of transformation, Mahadeva and Parvati decided to transform Mount Kraunch into their abode. This decision, driven by both admiration and love for their son, manifested in the creation of a *jyotirlinga* on the very spot where Kartikeya had initially immersed himself in penance.

The *jyotirlinga*, a symbol of their joint presence and eternal connection with Kartikeya, became a testament to the unbreakable bonds of familial love and the deep spiritual journey that each member of the deific family undertook in their own unique way.

Thus, Mallikarjuna came into existence. 'Mallika' connotes Parvati and 'Arjuna' connotes Shiva.

It is believed that Lord Shiva makes an appearance every *amavasya* (new moon), and Goddess Parvati makes her appearance every *purnima* (full moon) to catch a glimpse of their treasured son at Mount Kraunch.

*Some folklores state that Kartikeya went off to Mount Kraunch* because he was agitated after hearing that his brother Ganesha was getting married before him.

When their sons, Kartikeya and Ganesha, had come of age, Lord Shiva and Goddess Parvati decided to find suitable brides for them. In order to decide which of their beloved sons was to get married first, they announced that whichever son would first circumambulate the world thrice would be married first. When Ganesha traversed around his parents three times, proclaiming that his parents were his world, a dejected and embarrassed Kartikeya set off to Mount Kraunch. While Ganesha was married to the twins Riddhi and Siddhi, Kartikeya made Mount Kraunch his abode and took up the name of Kumarabrahmachari.

The temple of Srisailam is nestled away atop the Nallamalla hill range in Andhra Pradesh. It is dedicated to Mallikarjuna. The unique feature of this temple is the coexistence of a *jyotirlinga* and a *shaktipeetha*, a sacred site for the worship of Goddess Parvati Mahashakti, in the temple complex. This feature is rare, making the sacred location the humble abode of Lord Shiva and his consort, Goddess Parvati.

Mallikarjuna is the second *jyotirlinga*.

# MAHAKALESHWAR

## Unwavering Faith amid Chaos

*Avantikayam vihita-vataram*
*Mukti-pradanaya cha sajjananam*
*Akalamrityoh parirakshanartham*
*Vande maha-kala-maha-suresham*

I salute that Maha Kala
Who is the Lord of all *devas*
Who has incarnated in the city of Avanti
For giving salvation to good people
And to save people from untimely death.

In the serene embrace of the quaint little town of Avantikapuri resided a pious man named Vedapriya. Synonymous with his name, Vedapriya was a devout brahmin who dedicated his existence to the worship of Mahadeva. Each day, Vedapriya's prayers mingled with the hustle and bustle of Avantikapuri's streets, creating a melodious chorus that had become familiar to all. The denizens of the town had grown accustomed to and now looked forward to starting their day with these resounding chants.

He had four sons – Devapriya, Medhapriya, Sukrit and Dharmabahu. Infused with memories of their father's zealous piousness, the brothers found themselves enveloped in an atmosphere steeped in the fragrance of incense. Their father served as the guiding light, lovingly fostering their shared reverence for Mahadeva, where the sons, wide-eyed and curious, witnessed the sacred dances of fire and the melodic cadence of Vedic hymns.

Devapriya, the eldest, assumed the mantle of responsibility, absorbing the nuances of each ritual with diligence. Medhapriya, of thoughtful demeanour, immersed himself in the intellectual facets of their sacred traditions. Sukrit, the spirited one, approached each prayer with infectious enthusiasm, adding his unique touch to the sacraments performed. Dharmabahu, the youngest, observed with innocent wonder, absorbing the essence of steadfast obedience and sincerity towards the higher beings.

Their father, Vedapriya, was not just a parent but a living embodiment of reverence, instilling in them the values of humility, gratitude and steady faith. The brothers, like saplings nurtured by the same spiritual soil, flourished under the benevolent shade of their father's teachings. The town of Avantikapuri became a sacred ground where the sons explored the depths of their spirituality, each step embracing the footprints of generations past.

Impressed by Vedapriya's steadfast piety, Mahadeva bestowed abundant blessings upon him, ensuring him a life filled with contentment and grace. These sanctified benedictions paved the way for a synchronized existence, where the sacred threads of spirituality intertwined with the fabric of everyday life.

After the inevitable departure of Vedapriya from the mortal plane, his legacy lived on through the dutiful hands and devout hearts of his four sons. They carried forth the torch of tradition with untiring commitment, which defined their upbringing. Mahadeva, witness to this unbroken chain of veneration, observed as the brothers continued to illuminate the path of righteousness and spiritual aptitude.

Upon the formidable mountain of Ratanak, an *asura* named Dushan established his dominion. A devotee of unparalleled zeal, Dushan's allegiance lay with Lord Brahma, whom he worshipped fervently.

In the solitude of his austere abode, Dushan immersed himself in relentless penance, seeking the gracious favour of Lord Brahma. Shrouded in the clouds, the flowing pulse of Dushan's prayers swept through the peaks. His piety carved a pathway for the esoteric to manifest, and finally, the golden chariot of Lord Brahma, drawn by majestic white swans, graced the *asura*'s presence.

As Lord Brahma materialized, his commanding voice thundered, disrupting the tranquillity of Dushan's meditative state. The *asura*, pulled away from his contemplation, found himself in the awe-inspiring presence of his revered deity.

'Dushan!' Lord Brahma's words reverberated through the mountainous expanse. 'I am immensely impressed by your devout worship of me. Tell me, my beloved devotee, what boon must I grant you?'

Overwhelmed by the receptive acknowledgement, Dushan prostrated himself before Lord Brahma, expressing his gratitude before articulating his earnest desire. 'O Lord! I am blessed to behold your glorious form with my very eyes. Please bestow upon me insurmountable strength and power, my Lord.'

In response to the *asura*'s request, Lord Brahma, the Creator of the Universe, uttered the words that would shape Dushan's destiny. 'So be it,' he blessed Dushan, granting him the formidable might he sought. With that, Lord Brahma disappeared into the ethereal dimension, leaving behind a transformed *asura* on the mountain of Ratanak.

In the wake of his insatiable hunger for power, the now invincible Dushan embarked on a ruthless campaign of terror, spreading mayhem, and encouraging his fellow *asuras* to partake in looting and pillaging hapless villages on *bhu loka*. These once-tranquil landscapes fell prey to the marauding forces led by Dushan, who revelled in the conquest of vast territories, leaving a trail of devastation in his wake.

In a twist of fate, the *asuras*, under Dushan's command, targeted the little town of Avantikapuri with unbridled fury, ransacking its modest riches and instilling fear in the hearts of its inhabitants. The army of *asuras*, under the command of the power-hungry Dushan, descended upon Avantikapuri like a dark storm, leaving chaos and destruction in its wake. The once-serene streets resounded with the clamour of the marauding forces as they set about their nefarious acts.

Houses, once standing proudly, were now reduced to smouldering rubble as the *asuras* plundered them of their possessions and set aflame their very foundations. The air hung thick with the acrid odour of burning wood and the mournful cries of the helpless townspeople. The once-vibrant town square became a battleground, where the *asuras* revelled in their merciless conquest. Market stalls were overturned, goods were strewn haphazardly and the remnants of the thriving community were trampled upon by the callous invaders.

Roads that had witnessed the joyous hustle and bustle of everyday life now bore the scars of relentless brutality. *Asura* warriors, fuelled by avarice and aggression, rampaged through the streets, leaving destruction in their wake. The intricate patterns of the once-charming pathways were now marred by the footprints of malevolence.

The people of Avantikapuri, unsuspecting victims of this onslaught, fled in terror as their homes and belongings were laid to waste. The *asuras* left behind a desolate landscape of shattered dreams and scattered lives.

However, there remained one bastion of resistance – the land owned by the four brothers, Devapriya, Medhapriya, Sukrit and Dharmabahu. Refusing to yield their sacred land to the *asura* menace, the brothers stood firm in their conviction, resolute in their worship of Lord Shiva.

Undeterred by the mayhem unfolding around them, the brothers continued their intercession to the heavens, seemingly oblivious to the unrestrained fury of the *asura* armies. As the *asuras* approached their sanctuary, the brothers remained immersed in their prayers, paying no heed to the orders of the wrathful adversaries.

Outside, the *asuras*, angry and frustrated, grew increasingly impatient. The rhythmic sounds of bells and the soft murmurs of mantras seemed to create an invisible barrier, shielding the brothers from the impending danger just beyond their doorstep.

Dushan was infuriated by the brothers' disregard for his commands. His booming voice thundered, 'I have defeated great sages and the *devas*, ousting them from their positions of power. How can these lowly brahmins remain unperturbed by my campaign?'

Undeterred, the brothers continued their worship, their eyes closed in deep meditation.

Dushan's frustration was evident as he issued an ultimatum to them: 'If you wish to live, you must forsake your prayers to Shiva and rise to worship me!'

The *asuras* raised their weapons, ready to assail the praying brothers and shatter the tranquillity that enveloped their sacred space.

The villagers trembled in fear as they witnessed the impending clash between the devout brahmins and the belligerent *asuras*. 'O Brahmins,' they cried, 'please heed the words of the *asuras*. If you do not put a stop to your worship, they will slay us all.'

Devapriya looked into the fear-stricken eyes of the villagers and said, 'We do not have any weapons to counter the attack of the *asuras*. Only Mahadeva can save us now.' There was not a crease of worry on his face as he went back to his prayers to their ever-loving Lord.

The *asuras* could no longer contain their frustration. 'Enough of waiting for these wretched brahmins,' Dushan declared loudly. 'It is better that we teach them a lesson for disobeying the word of the greatest *asura* to have ever lived!' he bellowed as he hurtled towards them.

It was in this very moment that Mahadeva, the Cosmic Observer, chose to unveil His omniscient presence. A mysterious energy surrounded the brahmin brothers, as if the very fabric of reality shifted to accommodate His intervention. No force, mortal or otherwise, should dare disrupt the sanctity of His devout believers and their communion with the omnipresent.

A deafening explosion rocked the very foundations of Avantikapuri as the aura of Mahadeva surged into existence. With a thunderous roar, the mighty Lord materialized in a blaze of otherworldly brilliance. *Trishul* gripped firmly, He emerged as a benevolent guardian, positioning Himself boldly between the praying brahmins and the encroaching *asuras*. The trident gleamed with heavenly radiance, and an electric charge filled the atmosphere. The *asuras*, caught off guard by the sheer ferocity of Mahadeva's arrival, recoiled in fear.

'I am Mahakala!' bellowed Mahadeva, His wrath evident. 'I am here to protect my devotees, who are worshipping me! I shall rid the world of sinful creatures such as you. Leave the brahmins alone to complete their rituals, or face death at my hands!'

The air crackled with energy as the trident swirled in the celestial dance of destruction. Mahadeva defended His devoted worshippers with a display of unparalleled prowess. Each strike of the trident sent shockwaves through the astral realms, turning the confrontation into a spectacle of esoteric power and retribution. The *asuras*, stubborn in their defiance, were swiftly annihilated by the mighty Mahadeva, the indomitable force standing before them.

After swiftly dispatching the *asuras*, Mahadeva turned His attention to Dushan. Unyielding in the face of Brahma's boons, the Lord of Destruction confronted the *asura* with resolute determination. In a galactic showdown, Mahadeva brought an end to Dushan's reign of terror, dispelling the shadows of fear that had enveloped the land and its people.

With the demise of Dushan, a palpable shift occurred in the atmosphere of Avantikapuri. The air, recently ominous due to the presence of the *asuras*, once again lightened with joy. The battlefield transformed into a sacred space, marked by the exultant victory of Mahadeva. The brothers witnessed the transformation in awe, their hands folded as they bowed reverentially to their Lord.

Returning to the worshipping brothers, Mahadeva's countenance softened, radiating a calming energy. The brothers chanted His praises in unison, their voices echoing, 'Har Har Mahadeva!' Tears of pure happiness streamed down their faces, awash with the sanctity of the moment and the all-consuming presence before them.

Impressed by their deep fealty, Mahadeva spoke in a soothing tone, offering to fulfil their every request. As one, the brothers expressed their concentrated wish to break free from the cycle of life and desires, karma, and merge their existence with the divine essence of Mahadeva.

'So be it,' declared Mahadeva, His words echoing. In response to their heartfelt plea, the discernible energy transformed the very ground on which they stood. The tumultuous battleground morphed into a symbol of eternal worship - the sacred phallic structure, the *lingam*. This marked the inception of Mahakaleshwar, a living testament to Mahadeva's protection of His devotees and an enduring source of spiritual solace.

*Another story pertaining to the origin and greatness of* Mahakaleshwar revolves around the king of Ujjain, Chandrasena. A devout follower of Mahadeva, the king possessed a unique and extraordinary gem named *chintamani*. This lustrous stone, a gift from his adviser Manibhadra, had the remarkable ability to turn anything it touched into gold. Wearing this magical gem around his neck, King Chandrasena himself radiated a brilliant lustre, making him the envy of all other kings.

The brilliance of *chintamani* caught the attention of neighbouring rulers, stoking jealousy among them. Driven by greed, they plotted to obtain the miraculous gemstone for themselves. Kings Ripudamana and Singhaditya, leaders of rival armies, besieged the kingdom of Ujjain, surrounding King Chandrasena.

Trapped and facing the threat of war against two cunning adversaries, King Chandrasena turned to Mahadeva for His guidance.

Amid this dire situation, a mother and her infant son named Shrikhar, devout followers of Mahadeva, were passing through the area. Witnessing the plight of King Chandrasena, young Shrikhar began fervently praying to Mahadeva, seeking a timely intervention.

Impressed by the sincere prayers of the young devotee, Mahadeva appeared before Shrikhar and his mother in full glory. The revered presence blessed the mother and child, infusing the atmosphere with a renewed vitality. News of this astounding appearance reached the rival rulers, who, aware of King Chandrasena's deep homage to Mahadeva, decided to retreat immediately.

Fearful of invoking Mahadeva's wrath by causing distress to His devotees, the rival kings abandoned their siege. The miraculous intervention of Mahadeva, spurred by the innocent prayers of a child, averted the impending war, and secured the safety of King Chandrasena and his exquisite gem, thus reinforcing the belief that in time of need, Mahadeva will always come to the aid of those devoted to Him.

*In an alternative version of the tale, as young Shrikhar began* his earnest prayers to Mahadeva, the news of his plea reached the ears of a devoted priest named Vridhi. Deeply moved by the child's innocent and sincere submission, Vridhi also commenced his prayers to Mahadeva on the banks of the sacred River Kshipra.

However, despite the collective prayers, the kings Ripudamana and Singhaditya proved successful in their multipronged attack on the city. Their conquest was further aided by the malevolent *asura* Dushan, who possessed the boon of invisibility granted by Lord Brahma. The combined forces of the kings and demons wreaked havoc upon the city, terrorizing the inhabitants.

Upon witnessing the distress of His beloved devotees and the city's plight, Mahadeva descended from His imperturbable abode on Mount Kailasha. In a fierce and swift intervention, He confronted and slayed the *asura* and the malevolent kings who had orchestrated the assault.

Responding to the fervent pleas of young Shrikhar, the priest Vridhi and other devoted souls, Mahadeva, moved by their faith, manifested Himself as the Mahakaleshwar *jyotirlinga*. This altruistic act not only ended the threat to Ujjain but also established Mahadeva's sacred presence in the form of the *jyotirlinga*, offering solace and protection to His devotees for generations to come.

'*Maha*' means great, and '*kal*' means time, signifying time eternal, associated with and embodying the destructive aspect of time, and the eternal cycle of creation, preservation and destruction. Therefore, Mahakaleshwar refers to the greatness of Mahadeva, who appeared to protect His devotees when they needed Him the most.

The Mahakaleshwar *jyotirlinga* is situated in Ujjain, Madhya Pradesh.

It is the third *jyotirlinga*.

# OMKARESHWAR
## A Mountain's Wish for Glory

*Kaverika-narmadayoh pavitre*
*Samagame sajjana-taranaya*
*Sadaiva-mandha-tripure vasantam*
*Omkarameesham shivameka-meede*

He, who lives in Mandhatripura
Near the holy confluence
Of the rivers Cauvery and Narmada
To aid good people traverse
The Ocean of *Samsara*
On that peerless, benevolent Shiva
I meditate with the form of Om.

Vindhya reached skyward with unparalleled grandeur, her verdant slopes bedecked with dense forests that created a captivating contrast against the surrounding rugged terrain. Lush greenery, teeming with diverse life forms, painted a picture of abundant bounty and vitality, while the mountain herself stood as a towering testament to nature's magnificence.

The travelling musician and son of Brahma, Narada Muni, once decided to grace Vindhya with his presence. Dressed in saffron robes, his locks in a topknot, as he approached her with his golden veena in one hand and his *khartal* in the other, she could hear 'Narayana! Narayana!', which could only signify the announcement of his arrival. Vindhya received him with due pomp and splendour, fit for a being of his stature.

Narada, with a mischievous twinkle in his eyes, spoke of the wonders he had witnessed during his travels across the many worlds. He recounted tales of unimaginable beings, mystical arenas, and the eternal dance of creation, preservation and destruction that unfolded under the watchful gaze of the holy Trinity. Vindhya, in turn, listened in wonderment to Narada's fascinating anecdotes.

As the recapitulation and feasting concluded, Narada, his veena still expelling euphonious melodies, deduced that it was almost time to continue on his voyage. Known for provoking others and causing conflicts for his own amusement, he chose to broach a delicate topic before his departure. He started to sigh dramatically, laden with theatrics, intending to catch Vindhya's attention and lure her into his carefully devised trap. Vindhya, observant and vigilant, enquired after the departing sage just as he expected, sensing something was amiss, 'Narada Muni! What is the matter? Are you feeling unwell?'

With a sly smile and the musical jingle of his *khartal*, Narada addressed Vindhya, 'Narayana, Narayana. Vindhya, I was traversing the three worlds when I felt a calling to visit you after a considerable time. However, that is not the sole reason for my presence before you today.'

The wicked twinkle in Narada's eyes grew more pronounced as he smoothly moved to a sensitive topic. Vindhya waited expectantly to hear what he had to say.

In a spirited tone, Narada began to share gossip that had reached his ears about Mount Sumeru being considered greater than Vindhya. Instantly taking the bait, Vindhya proudly responded, 'It is impossible. I am much greater than Mount Sumeru and taller too. Everyone knows that.'

Narada, still wearing his tricksy smirk, contradicted, 'No, no, no. The consensus is that Mount Sumeru is greater and taller than you.' His words were carefully chosen to provoke an uncharacteristic response from the majestic mountain.

Vindhya, now concerned about her stature, had unknowingly fallen into the snare set by Narada. The sage, revelling in the amusement he derived from such repartee, continued, 'I tried conveying this truth to whoever would listen, but alas, my efforts were in vain. My sighs, dear Vindhya, were an involuntary expression of concern for your diminishing stature. I could not bear to keep this troubling information from you!'

Having achieved his purpose quite adequately, he thought, Narada sauntered away, leaving Vindhya in an abyss of self-doubt and confusion. As a parting note, he said, 'Do not worry; I, for one, still consider you the greatest and tallest. But, alas, we cannot deny that Sumeru, is one among the *devas* - even Surya circumambulates Sumeru, but not you. Narayana! Narayana!' Speaking thus, Narada Muni walked away, satisfied with the subterfuge that was now afoot.

In the silence that followed Narada's departure, Vindhya wrestled with newfound insecurities. The proud mountain began to question her own towering prominence and might, along the valleys of self-pity. The revelation that Mount Sumeru, one among the *devas*, held a perceived superiority haunted Vindhya's thoughts.

'Am I not the greatest mountain?' she lamented. Her hurt ego, meticulously predicted by Narada, wrapped her in a cloak of melancholia.

Determined to reclaim her greatness, Vindhya swore to alter the baseless narrative. 'I must find a way to command Surya's brilliance. If the Sun God showers his radiance upon me, I will stand unmatched, the supreme being among mountains.'

Her determination to refute Narada's words drove a new purpose. 'I shall surpass Sumeru in height, strength and grandeur,' she proclaimed, a silent vow to herself. 'I will be the unequivocal superior.' Saying thus, and recognizing that winning the favour of the greatest of gods was her best recourse, she resolved to do whatever it took to secure an audience with Him.

Through the passing months of untiring reverence, Vindhya's penance reached a crescendo that carried across *lokas*. Lord Shiva, drawn by the sincerity of Vindhya's efforts, decided to manifest and fulfil the mountain's fervent desire.

One day, as the sun dipped below the horizon and the intensity of Vindhya's penance grew stronger, Lord Shiva materialized before her. The sacred ambience of Amreshwar, the chosen site of her adulation, was engulfed with primordial energy, and Vindhya, humbled and overjoyed, prostrated herself before the deity.

'Vindhya,' Lord Shiva spoke, His voice matching the tenor of the cosmos. 'I am pleased with your unstinting devoutness. Rise, and state your desire, for I am inclined to grant it.'

Vindhya, her heart pounding with anticipation, arose and looked into the eyes of the Lord for the first time. With bated breath, she spoke, 'O Mahadeva, the greatest among the gods, I seek to be greater than Mount Sumeru. Grant me this boon, so I may stand unmatched even among my equals.'

With a serene countenance, Lord Shiva addressed Vindhya, 'I will grant you what you desire. You shall be considered greater and taller than Mount Sumeru, and your growth shall know no bounds. However, in return, you must make a solemn promise – you shall never inconvenience anybody with your endowments and will rely on them delicately.'

The omniscient Mahadeva, aware of the potential consequences of the boon, delivered caution with a sense of foreboding. He understood Vindhya's insecure nature as well as her unassuming intentions and foresaw the challenges that might arise from the mountain's unbridled growth. Still, once a boon is spoken, it becomes an unalterable component of the hermetic design, and so, He deigned to let the occurrence run its course.

Lord Shiva, with abstruse wisdom, continued, 'Use this gift wisely, Vindhya. Let your greatness be a symbol of sublime grace, not a source of distress for others. Promise me that you will uphold the sanctity of this boon.'

Vindhya, elated by the boon and eager to showcase her newfound greatness, readily agreed: 'O Mahadeva, I am grateful for your benevolence. I promise to obey you and follow your guidance. I will heed your warnings without hesitation.'

With Vindhya's earnest assurances, Lord Shiva bestowed the boon, setting in motion the unceasing growth of the mountain. Mahadeva's eyes held hints of hope and concern for recondite balance.

No sooner had the words left His lips than a surge of elemental energy enveloped Vindhya, infusing her with strength and grandeur. The mountain, once overshadowed by doubts, now stood transformed, ready to claim its place as the unparalleled colossus among a cohort of peers.

Vindhya, elated, bowed before Lord Shiva. 'Thank you, O Mahadeva, I shall forever be indebted to Your benevolence.'

With a gentle smile, Lord Shiva blessed Vindhya, 'May your greatness shine through the ages, and may your earnestness endure. Rise, Vindhya, and let the world witness your splendour.'

Emboldened by the boon, Vindhya descended from Amreshwar, now a mountain of unmatched stature, fulfilling her quest for supremacy. The exchange between Mahadeva and Vindhya marked a pivotal moment in the relationship between a devotee and her deity, where zeal had the power to reshape destinies.

Vindhya, though cognizant of the inconvenience her power could cause, became intoxicated with pride and obstinately refused to heed or accommodate others' needs. She persisted in towering over everyone and everything, gradually relegating her promise to

Mahadeva to the recesses of her memory, and eventually forgetting it altogether. When attempts were made to reason with her, she dismissed them with laughter, her unchecked dominance over the realms clouding her judgement, and revealing ugly shades of insecurity and arrogance, as anticipated by Narada Muni when he set these events in motion.

In the wake of Vindhya's unrelenting growth, trouble loomed over the *lokas*. Her immense ascent began to cast shadows over the sun, obstructing his radiant light, and the moon too found himself veiled by the ever-expanding mountain. Disturbed by this upheaval of the natural order, the affected beings sought a solution.

The wise and revered Sage Agastya, a *saptarishi* and ardent devotee of Shiva, emerged as their beacon of hope. Aware of his prowess and ability to navigate such inscrutable challenges, the deities approached Agastya with their plea for respite from Vindhya's unrestrained growth.

Crafting a remedy, he approached the colossal Vindhya and conveyed his intention to undertake a pilgrimage.

'Great Vindhya,' he began, 'I come before you with a humble plea. I am about to embark on a sacred pilgrimage, and I beseech you to cease your relentless growth until my return.'

Vindhya, mighty and unyielding, loomed overhead, her craggy peaks piercing the sky.

'Why should I heed your request, O sage?' she rumbled. 'I have grown accustomed to reaching for the skies, and my ascent knows no bounds.'

Undeterred by the mountain's defiance, Sage Agastya maintained his composure, unflinching as he spoke. 'I understand your desire, noble mountain,' he replied calmly, 'but my pilgrimage is of the utmost importance, and your ceaseless rise may disrupt the accord of the land. Please, for the sake of all beings and the fruitful completion of my pilgrimage, grant me this favour.'

A moment of silence passed between them, heavy as the mist enveloping them. Then, with a rumble that shook the earth beneath their feet, Vindhya spoke once more.

'Very well, revered sage,' she said, her voice softer now, touched by a hint of reverence. 'For the sake of your pilgrimage and out of respect for your earnest plea, I shall abide by your request. May your journey be blessed.'

And so, with a solemn nod of gratitude, Sage Agastya and his wife departed, leaving behind the towering mountain in a state of temporary dormancy.

The sage cleverly decided to settle in Srisailam and never return, and Vindhya, true to her promise, ceased to grow. However, Lord Shiva, cognizant of the need for perpetual vigilance, installed Himself in the form of two *lingas*. One *linga* took the name Amreshwar, and the other became known as Omkareshwar, symbolizing His presence to sanctify the turbulent history of the land.

This ensured that Vindhya remained bound by the primaeval will and that the boon bestowed upon her would not be misused again.

The balance of the quarter, disrupted by Vindhya's unchecked aspirations, found resolution through the collective intervention of sages, deities and the will of Lord Shiva.

The two *lingas*, Omkareshwar and Amreshwar, stand eternal witnesses to the events that unfolded, symbolizing the triumph of astute wisdom over unchecked power.

Narada Muni watched from afar, an impish grin spreading across his face. He could not help but chuckle heartily, revelling in the entertaining repercussions of his mischievous endeavours.

*A lesser known but intriguing version of the origin of* Omkareshwar unfolds a tale of supernatural conflict and divine intervention. In a time when the *deva*s and *asura*s clashed in yet another battle for supremacy, the scales tipped ominously in favour of the *asura*s, leaving the *deva*s in despair.

The *devas*, in their darkest hour, turned to the resolute deity, Lord Shiva, seeking liberation from the onslaught of the *asura*s. The Lord of Destruction, moved by their distress, decided to intervene.

On the battlefield, where the clash of comparable forces had plunged the cosmos into chaos, Lord Shiva manifested His imposing presence. In a resplendent display of confounding power, He transformed into Omkareshwar – the embodiment of the sacred syllable 'Om', resonating with the primordial sound of creation.

Omkareshwar, a formidable force of energy, surged into the heart of the conflict, confronting the *asura*s with vigour. The battlefield became an arena where godly and demonic forces clashed in an epic struggle for supremacy.

The thunderous sound of Lord Shiva's *damaru* – the double-sided, hourglass-shaped drum, the embodiment of the rhythm of the Universe – pierced through the tumult of battle, signalling the beginning of His intervention. With trident in hand, Omkareshwar unleashed a torrent of energy, striking fear into the hearts of the *asura*s. The battlefield became a canvas for the riveting dance of destruction, enacted by Lord Shiva Himself.

In the subsequent onslaught, Omkareshwar vanquished the *asura*s, dismantling their forces and restoring balance in the Universe. The victory of the *deva*s was sealed, and once again, order prevailed over the agents of chaos.

As the echoes of battle subsided, the victorious *deva*s expressed their gratitude to Lord Shiva, recognizing Omkareshwar as the sacred symbol of their triumph. The tangible manifestation of Omkareshwar became a symbol of hope, a testament to the fundamental order of the Universe.

*Another version of the origin of Omkareshwar traces the sacred* saga of King Mandhata and his devout sons, whose single-minded dedication led to the manifestation of the holy *linga*s at the revered site of Omkareshwar.

King Mandhata, a noble monarch of times past, ruled with wisdom and virtue. His pledge to Lord Shiva was unparalleled, setting the stage for a saga that would ring true across the vast expanses of time. Alongside him were his two sons, both the epitome of piety and ardent worship.

Driven by an insatiable yearning to connect with the supernatural, the king and his sons embarked on a spiritual journey, delving into the formidably distinguished stages of penance and *yagna*s dedicated to Lord Shiva. Their austere practices and resolute commitment stirred inexplicable energies, drawing the attention of the Supreme Being.

Pleased by the sincere endeavours of King Mandhata and his sons, Lord Shiva chose to grace them with His hypnotic presence. In a mystical flourish, Mahadeva, the eternal essence, gracefully unveiled the manifestation of His sacred presence in the form of two resplendent *linga*s, casting a radiant aura of transcendence and spiritual luminescence upon the revered grounds of Omkareshwar. These embodiments of Shiva's transcendental energy became objects of veneration and a source of intimate connection for devotees.

The story of King Mandhata and his sons, engraved in the sacred tapestry of Omkareshwar, stands as a testament to the transformative power of devotion. It reflects the immutable interplay between mortal aspiration and everlasting grace, etching a sacred narrative that continues to inspire the faithful on their spiritual quests.

Shivpuri is an island with two temples, one for the Omkareshwar *linga* and the other for the Amreshwar *linga*. As the island of Shivpuri seems to be in the shape of the sacred 'ॐ', the temple was named 'Omkareshwar'.

The temple of Omkareshwar is situated on the banks of the River Narmada at Mandhata (Shivpuri), Madhya Pradesh.

It is the fourth *jyotirlinga*.

# KEDARESHWAR

## The Fervent Devotion of the Twins

*Mahadri-parshve cha tate ramantam*
*Sampujyamanam satatam muneendreh*
*Surasureyr-yaksha-mahoragadhyeh,*
*Kedarameesham shivameka-meede*

He, who resides close to the great mountain
Who is ever worshipped by the great sages
And by *devas*, *asuras*, *yakshas* and *nagas*
On that benign Lord of Kedara
I meditate.

Twins Nara and Narayana, the fourth avatar of Lord Vishnu, descended to earth as part of their sacred mission to safeguard and foster the welfare of humanity. Their earthly origin traces back to Dharma, the son of Lord Brahma, and Murti, the daughter of Daksha Prajapati.

Choosing the guise of austere sages, Nara and Narayana embarked on a noble journey to devote themselves to the betterment of humankind. Their abode was the serene land of Badrika, where they dedicated their time to exacting austerities and deep meditation, channelling their exuberant energies for the greater good of the world.

Every day, with complete dedication, the twins embarked on rigorous penance at the hallowed Badrikashram. For their devout practice, they meticulously crafted a *lingam* out of sand and reverently worshipped it. Their sonorous prayers reached the heavens, catching the attention of Mahadeva, who observed their steadfast commitment closely.

Drawn by the sheer consistency and intensity of their piety, He decided to grace them with His presence.

'Nara and Narayana,' He said, 'I am pleased by your dedication and the noble purpose that drives your actions. Ask of me a boon, and I shall grant it.'

Humbled by the opportunity to beget a boon from the Lord Himself, Nara and Narayana, with utmost sincerity, expressed their true, heartfelt desire.

'Mahadeva, we would be beholden to you to take permanent abode on the sacred grounds of Badrikashram. With your grace, may this idyllic place become a haven where devotees can visit and worship you, ensuring the continuous flow of blessings for the well-being of all.'

Touched by their selfless allegiance and the noble purpose behind their request, Mahadeva granted their wish. Kedareshwar, a manifestation of the metaphysical, emerged on that very spot, marking the culmination of the twins' dedication and the establishment of a holy pilgrimage site for generations to come.

Thus, Kedareshwar was actualized.

*In another version of this tale, in the aftermath of the devastating Kurukshetra* war, the Pandavas, burdened by the weight of guilt and the stains of their familial bloodshed, sought redemption. With heavy hearts and a gnawing sense of remorse, the Pandavas – Yudhishthira, Arjuna, Bhima, Sahadeva and Nakula – approached Lord Shiva, seeking vindication for the sins committed during the cataclysmic war.

Lord Shiva, unwilling to condone their actions, assumed the form of a bull to evade them. Guided by their elders' counsel, the five brothers set forth on a journey to locate the only preternatural being who could grant them solace and forgiveness.

So Lord Shiva, concealing His true identity, roamed through the changing territories, while the brothers pressed on in their pursuit of Him, determined to find the presence that could cleanse their souls of the sins that haunted them.

When they spotted Him, Mahadeva chose not to reveal His true form and dove underground to evade their pursuit. Unyielding, Bhima, the mightiest among the Pandavas, plunged after Him, managing to grasp only the hump of the bull.

Legend has it that the very spot where Bhima caught hold of the bull's hump became the sacred sanctuary of Kedareshwar. The presence of Lord Shiva, concealed beneath the earth, transformed this location into a symbol of redemption and forgiveness. The other body parts of the bull, representing Him, manifested in the surrounding areas, marking the sanctity of the entire region. The navel emerged in Madhya-Maheshwar, the forelegs in Tunganath, the face in Rudranath and the hair in Kalpeshwar. These five holy spots are often collectively referred to as the 'Panch Kedar'.

*In another captivating legend, the sacred land of Kedareshwar* holds the essence of Devi Parvati's yearning for union with Lord Shiva in their *ardhanarishwara* form. The evocative narrative unfolded as Devi Parvati embarked on a reflective journey of worship and penance dedicated to Lord Shiva.

In response to Devi Parvati's devoted worship, He manifested Himself as Kedareshwar, presenting the unique and awe-inspiring form of *ardhanarishwara*. This endowed union, where

Lord Shiva and Devi Parvati become one, in a harmonious blend of masculine and feminine energies, symbolizes the inseparable and complementary forces of creation.

The Kedareshwar Temple is located in the lower Himalayas on the banks of the River Mandakini (and the mystical Saraswati) in the Rudraprayag district of Uttarakhand.

It is the fifth *jyotirlinga*.

# BHIMASHANKAR

## A Quest for Revenge

*Yam dakini-shakinika-samaje*
*Nishevyamanam pishita-shanaishcha*
*Sadaiva bhimadi-pada-prasiddham*
*Tam shankaram bhakta-hitam namami*

He, who is revered by *rakshasas*
In the company of the spirits named Dakini and Shakini
To him – Bhimshankar
Benefactor of believers
I bow in respect.

In the shadow of the Sahya mountains, a tragic tale unfolded, intertwining the destinies of Kumbhakarna, the brother of Ravana, the king of Lanka, and Karkati, the unsuspecting maiden who would give birth to Bhimasura.

Kumbhakarna, driven by the vigour of his reckless exploits for Lanka, encountered Karkati, a vulnerable maiden seeking refuge in the solitude of the mountains. The echoes of Kumbhakarna's forceful intrusion reverberated through the untouched valleys, leaving Karkati burdened with the seed of an unwanted union.

Fearing for the life of her unborn child amid the turmoil created by Ravana's pursuit of Sita, and the ensuing battle, Karkati sought refuge in the Sahya mountains. It was there, in the serene landscape, that she hoped to nurture and protect her yet unborn child from the blowout of Ravana's unscrupulous battles and the impending fall of Lanka.

Eventually, Kumbhakarna, along with many of his brothers and nephews, including Ravana, faced his demise in the final war against Shri Rama, leaving Karkati without any support or sustenance, carrying the weight of impending motherhood.

Bhimasura, a child born of contemptible beginnings, commenced his journey in the world, marked by the sins of his progenitor. Karkati, already burdened by the weight of unchosen motherhood, now faced the added challenge of raising a child conceived in the shadows of an abhorrent encounter. Despite the pain of her past, Karkati embraced her maternal role, determined to protect Bhimasura from the infamy of his lineage, steadfast in her decision to never set foot in Lanka. Becoming a shield for her son, she committed to never disclose to Bhimasura the unfortunate tale of his entry into the world.

Karkati, a loving mother, brought up her son Bhimasura in humble dwellings in the quiet embrace of the mountains, not calling for any attention, her son blissfully unaware of the circumstances surrounding his birth and the reason for their self-imposed isolation from the rest of the world.

Showering Bhimasura with all her affection, Karkati lived for her son and could see nothing beyond him. Their days were filled with shared laughter, play and the warmth of a mother's care; she taught her son all she knew about the world. Despite the idyllic life they led, Karkati harboured a deep-seated fear of the day her son would question the mysteries surrounding his birth.

The inevitable day arrived when Bhimasura, innocent and inquisitive, approached his mother, yearning to understand his lineage. His curiosity stirred the calm surface of their simple existence. 'Mother, I feel complete in your love, but I cannot help wondering about my father and his family, whom we have never known. Why do we live in seclusion on this mountain?' he implored.

Caught between the desire to safeguard her son from the unsettling truths of his ancestry and the inevitability of his queries, Karkati hesitated. The innocence reflected in Bhimasura's eyes tugged at her heart, and she struggled with the decision to relive her painful past.

Ultimately, she chose honesty, breaking the promise to herself. 'My dear son, your father was Kumbhakarna, a formidable *asura* and the younger brother of Ravana, then ruler of Lanka,' she began. 'Despite the path of *adharma* chosen by Ravana, your father fought in the war against Shri Rama, the incarnation of Narayana. Tragically, your father met his end on the battlefield.'

In great detail, Karkati unfolded the chapters of the war, revealing the complexities and consequences that defined Bhimasura's lineage.

Young and hot-blooded, Bhimasura, upon learning the tumultuous history of his birth, found himself engulfed in a seething rage. He started to believe that Rama was the reason he would never experience a father's love. The tales of the war and the account of the fall of his father at the hands of Rama, filled him with an intense desire for vengeance. No longer an affable denizen of the Sahya mountains, Bhimasura became a cauldron of anger and resentment.

Karkati, witnessing the transformation of her son, felt concern mount within her. Her pleas for him to embrace a life of peace fell on deaf ears, drowned out by his burgeoning fury. The near-perfect existence of mother and son became shadowed by the storm of emotions swirling within Bhimasura's fiery heart. In the solitude of the mountains, the seeds of reprisal took root, and Karkati could only watch, praying for her son's well-being amid the rising tempest of his emotions.

The clash between the *vanara* army of Rama and the *asura* forces of Ravana unfolded in a series of strategic manoeuvres and devastating losses on both sides. The *vanaras* fought valiantly, and as the conflict escalated, Ravana's army found itself dwindling, suffering more significant losses than their adversaries.

In a desperate attempt to turn the tide, Ravana resorted to regain his mighty brother, Kumbhakarna, from *nidra loka*. In Ravana's bid to awaken his brother, a clamourous cacophony of thunderous drums echoed, reverberating through the calm dominions of sleep. The loud beats were accompanied by the tantalizing aroma of freshly prepared savoury dishes. Their fragrances wafted through the air, intended to reach the senses of the colossal *asura* and entice him into wakefulness. As the drums persisted and the appetizing scents invaded *nidra loka*, a gradual shift occurred in Kumbhakarna's restful domain. The gigantic figure stirred, responding to the orchestrated efforts to rouse him from his extended repose.

As Kumbhakarna slowly wakened from his deep slumber, the sounds of war reached his ears. As he became more aware of his surroundings, the *asura* realized that something was amiss and not all was well in his homeland.

His eyes widened as he comprehended the turmoil that had befallen his beloved Lanka. The trumpets signalled the ongoing battle at a near distance, and the redolence of home-cooked food became tainted with the odour of blood.

Kumbhakarna's mind raced to grasp the reality of the conflict. He saw the shadow of war stretching over the land he loved, threatening to consume everything in its path. Concern etched across his massive face, Kumbhakarna's thoughts turned to his brother, Ravana, the cause of the ongoing strife. A growing sense of responsibility and concern for his brother's safety and the suffering of his kin gripped his heart, prompting him to contemplate the role he must play in the unfolding spectacle.

'Ravana, my brother, what madness has befallen you?' Kumbhakarna thought.

'I must reason with him, bring an end to this carnage. Bloodshed cannot be the legacy of Lanka. I will do whatever it takes to protect my people.' Thinking thus, Kumbhakarna set forth, determined to confront Ravana and persuade him to reconsider his path. Little did he know that his awakening would mark a crucial turning point in the war that was raging.

Kumbhakarna, towering over the battlefield, approached Ravana with urgency. 'Brother, what folly has consumed you?' he implored. 'Our land is embroiled in chaos and suffering. We must end this bloodshed and seek the path of peace.'

However, Ravana's eyes glowed with determination, and his response was adamant. 'Peace, brother, is a luxury we cannot afford,' he declared, unmoved by Kumbhakarna's appeals. 'Lanka must assert its dominance, and I will not waver in my quest for power. Rama and his allies must be crushed.'

Despite Kumbhakarna's attempts to reason with his brother, Ravana's obstinacy prevailed. The massive *asura*, torn between his brotherly love for Ravana and the desire to avert further destruction, found himself reluctantly joining the battle on the side of the *asuras*.

As Kumbhakarna descended into the battlefield, the sheer force of his presence shifted the momentum in favour of the *asuras*. His mace, wielded with unparalleled skill, wreaked havoc among the *vanara* ranks. As he stomped on the smaller warriors, Kumbhakarna's thick-skinned body proved impervious to their attacks.

The *vanara* leaders roared their battle cries, rallying their forces against the mighty Kumbhakarna. Hanuman, the robust *vanara*, hurled a rugged monolith at the formidable warrior, his war cry echoing through the acrid air. 'Jai Shri Ram!' he bellowed, channelling the sagacious power of his lord.

The monolith, thrown with incredible force, pierced Kumbhakarna's chest, but the imposing *asura* pressed forward. Sugriva and Angada joined the fray, their call to arms blending with the roars of the *vanara* army. 'For Rama! For *dharma*!' they shouted, wielding their weapons against their adversary.

Rama, observing the futile attempts to subdue Kumbhakarna, knew that more decisive action was required. Iron-jawed, he aimed the *Vayavyastra*, an astral missile, at Kumbhakarna's right hand. The deadly arrow struck with precision, severing the colossal warrior's limb. Undeterred, Kumbhakarna roared in defiance, the bloodied stump raised high.

The *vanara* leaders, witnessing the unremitting determination of their enemy, continued their noble efforts. 'Hold strong! We fight for righteousness!' Angada shouted, rallying his comrades against the *asura*.

Sugriva boomed, 'With the grace of Shri Rama, we shall prevail!'

Rama, meanwhile, prepared for another strike. The *Vayavya,* once again unleashed with precision, severed Kumbhakarna's remaining arm. The battlefield quaked with the intensity of the battle cries, the clash of weapons and the blood-curdling roars of the combatants.

As the armless Kumbhakarna stood, a towering figure diminished by the onslaught, Rama's final arrow, ablaze with astral power, found its mark. With a searing intensity, the weapon pierced through the heart of the great warrior, whose overarching presence had temporarily shifted the tides of battle in the *asuras*' favour. Slowly, inexorably, Kumbhakarna began to topple, faltering under the weight of defeat. As he fell, the battlefield bore witness to the culmination of his rampant assault, a brief deafening silence descending upon the mayhem, broken only by the sickening thud of his collapse to the ground.

Karkati had known meagre bliss in her matrimony with Viradha. They eked out a living in the forest, where Viradha hunted for sustenance, and Karkati gathered the accompaniments for their paltry hunts. Their modest existence was shattered when Viradha met his demise, a tragedy that Karkati attributed to Rama's hand, during one of his hunting expeditions. She believed that her husband had perished by Rama's arrow, caught in an attempt to forage food for his family.

Faced with the grim reality of inadequate sustenance, Viradha had resolved to hunt a baby deer that he had stumbled upon, driven by the desperation of hunger. Despite his awareness that hunting down a newborn was abhorrent, hunger had clouded his judgement. It was in this dire moment that Rama had intervened, swiftly ending Viradha's misguided pursuit, to prevent him from harming the innocent foal.

With a heavy heart and unresolved grief, Karkati returned to live with her parents, Karkata and Pukasi. Karkati found solace in caring for her ageing parents in their small forest hut near the Sahya mountains. To survive, the family resorted to robbing passing travellers of their possessions, in the hope of finding adequate sustenance.

As days of starvation passed, the family's desperation reached its peak when they spotted a lone young man in saffron clothes passing by their derelict lodgings. Driven by hunger-induced delirium, they decided to rob him, oblivious to the fact that the man was Sutikshana, a disciple of the revered Sage Agastya, who had outsmarted Vindhya and limited her unencumbered growth, among other feats.

Sutikshana, on his way to reunite with his guru, was taken aback by the attack of the starving family. Anger welled up within him, and he cursed Karkati's parents, who were attempting to snatch his cloth bag. The curse took immediate effect, and the old, hungry couple dropped lifeless to the ground.

As Karkati's parents lay unmoving, Sutikshana turned his attention to Karkati, who had hidden herself. She trembled in the bushes, fear and remorse clouding her eyes. Sutikshana, his anger subsiding, shot her a pensive look. Speaking sternly, he said, 'You, lurking in the shadows, see what happens when desperation takes hold. Your parents paid a heavy price for their actions.'

Karkari rose, her voice trembling. 'Forgive us, noble sage. Hunger drove us mad. I never wanted harm to befall you or my parents.'

Sutikshana's tone softened. 'Hunger can push us to extremes, but consequences will follow. Your parents acted rashly, and now they are gone. You are still here. What will you make of this encounter-turned-ordeal?'

Karkati took a few moments to gather her thoughts and come to grips with the results of her actions. She looked around her to see the small, dilapidated hut that she shared with her parents and realized she had nothing else left in the world. 'I do not know, Revered One. I am alone, burdened by grief and guilt. How can I seek redemption?'

'Redemption lies in understanding consequences and choosing virtue. Reflect on the choices that led to this tragedy, and let them guide your path.'

The narrow forest path, flanked by towering trees, bore witness to Karkati's anguish. The sun-dappled leaves overhead seemed to flicker in empathy. 'I will, noble sage. But what about my parents? Can anything be done for them?'

'Their fate is sealed by the curse; I cannot reverse it. Yet, you can honour their memory by choosing a righteous path. Live a life that brings solace to their departed souls.'

With those words, Sutikshana continued his journey down the winding path, leaving Karkati standing alone. The sage's advice lingered like a gentle breeze, challenging her to find meaning and redemption amid tragedy.

It was only a few sombre days later that Kumbhakarna found his way to Karkati's meagre dwellings. . .

Hearing his mother's shocking revelation sent Bhimasura reeling. This changed the way he looked at his life, at the world and, in particular, at the *devas*. Karkati confessed, 'I always intended to shield you from this truth and ensure you lead an untroubled life, but out of a commitment to honesty, I have chosen to reveal it to you now.'

Bhimasura fell silent, and as the days passed by, his hatred for the *devas* began to grow. He stoked the fire of abhorrence within him as, in his head, he kept replaying the death of his father and the loss incurred by his dear mother at the hands of the *devas*.

He often thought to himself, 'It was not Rama who killed my father. It was Vishnu, in the guise of Rama, who killed my father! Rama is but a mere *manava*. The gods had to disguise themselves and come down to kill my infallible father and take away the strife-free life my mother was accustomed to. It was also by the hands of Vishnu that I lost my grandparents, and my mother lost her husband. So it is the *devas* who are to be blamed for our collective misfortune. It is because of them that I have been left fatherless and my mother without her family. I must avenge his death. I will avenge my father's death.'

Thus, Bhimasura became utterly indifferent to the idyllic life his mother had painstakingly crafted for him, which included his sheltered childhood. Instead of directing his attention to the present, and acknowledging the peace and protection bestowed upon him, he became engrossed in what he perceived as loss, despite having never experienced it first-hand.

Bhimasura's penance was a testament to his determination and thirst for revenge. Standing on one foot, atop a hill, he endured the harsh elements with eyes closed, focusing on the venerable Creator. The scorching sun mercilessly seared his skin, and the rain provided only momentary relief. Days melted into months as Bhimasura's unshakable resolve captured the attention of Lord Brahma.

Pleased with Bhimasura's tenacity, Brahma decided to make an appearance. 'Remarkable penance, my child. You have my attention now. What is it that you seek?'

Bhimasura, with fire in his eyes, replied, 'Grant me the power to avenge my father's death and bring havoc to the *devas*!'

Recognizing his resolve, Brahma granted Bhimasura the boon of insurmountable strength and power. 'Your wish is granted,' he declared, as a surge of energy enveloped Bhimasura. The mortal being now possessed an unassailable invincibility.

Driven by hatred and his newly acquired strength, Bhimasura could not wait to unleash chaos upon heaven and earth. As he flexed his muscles, he remarked, 'The *devas* will know the tribulations they brought upon themselves.'

The deities, sensing an impending storm, began to flee their palaces in fear. Indra, the king of gods, trembled as news of Bhimasura's indomitability spread. In a hushed conversation with his fellow deities, he murmured, 'We must find a way to deal with this enraged tyrant. His power is unlike anything we have faced before.'

The heavenly stage was thrown into disarray as Bhimasura's rampage began. The palaces echoed with the sounds of destruction. The preordained order was now in jeopardy, and the *devas* faced an adversary fortified by vengeance.

Amid Bhimasura's ruthless conquests, the majestic kingdom of Kamarupa fell victim to his tyranny. Among the countless victims was King Kamarupeshwara, captured and imprisoned in a constricted cell. The ruler found himself in a grim predicament, enclosed by the cold, damp walls of his prison.

In a state of despair and helplessness, King Kamarupeshwara turned to the one source of solace he believed could bring salvation – Lord Shiva. In the dim, oppressive confines of his prison, permeated by Bhimasura's malevolence, he embarked on a poignant spiritual journey.

With a heavy heart, he gathered whatever mud was available within his cell and fashioned a *lingam* in a cramped corner, a modest symbol of his unwavering faith in a higher order and his resilient spirit.

Day after day, King Kamarupeshwara fervently chanted the mantra '*Om Namah Shivaya!*' within his forced confines. The rhythmic repetition of the mantra became his lifeline, a plea for expedient intervention in the face of his captivity. In those solitary moments, with each utterance of the sacred words, he sought strength and the grace of Lord Shiva.

The king's wife, Dakshina, had managed to escape Bhimasura's clutches and sought refuge in hiding.

Despite the physical distance separating them, the couple remained deeply connected by their unwavering devotion to Lord Shiva.

In her secluded sanctuary, Dakshina, her heart heavy with worry and longing, fervently prayed to Mahadeva for her husband's safe return. Beside her, she fashioned a makeshift *lingam* from the soft sand, mirroring King Kamarupeshwara's reverence in his prison cell. Day after day, she too tirelessly chanted '*Om Namah Shivaya*!' before the sand-formed *lingam*, seeking solace and divine intervention.

The intertwined prayers of husband and wife, though separated by space, united through the vast expanse of the Universe. Their earnest plea reached the ears of Mahadeva, who, moved by their sincerity and shared suffering, decided to respond.

Only He could alter the course of Bhimasura's relentless rampage, and bring hope to the imprisoned king and his defenceless wife.

Amid the pandemonium, the *devas*, recognizing the dire need for propitious intervention, also moulded a *lingam* with reverence and began to offer their prayers.

Mahadeva, the Lord of Destruction and a benevolent deity, responded to the sincere litanies of His devotees. He materialized before the *devas*.

'You have called for me, and I have appeared. What is it that you want of me?' Mahadeva enquired obligingly,

His gaze sweeping over the worry-etched faces of the *devas*. The supernatural beings prostrated themselves before His feet.

'Mahadeva! Bhimasura is terrorizing our world and the others,' the *devas* lamented. 'Driven by a dangerous hatred towards us, he seeks to avenge the death of his father, the *asura* Kumbhakarna, at the hands of Lord Vishnu's avatar. Please, O Mahadeva, end Bhimasura's reign of terror and restore light to our world.'

'So be it,' pronounced Mahadeva, His voice an all-encompassing authority. With a nod, He vanished as swiftly as He had appeared, leaving behind a reassurance of peace.

Meanwhile, a dramatic turn of events unfolded within the prison where King Kamarupeshwara was held captive. Contorted news reached Bhimasura that the king, a devotee of Mahadeva, was casting dark spells to hasten his captor's demise. Enraged, Bhimasura raced to the prison cell, sword drawn, ready to spill blood and snuff out a life.

'What spells are you trying to cast on me, you wretched king?' Bhimasura screeched. King Kamarupeshwara, looking deferentially at the mud-formed *lingam*, calmly responded, 'I am worshipping Mahadeva. Only He can save me now.'

Bhimasura burst into hysterical laughter, mocking the king's beliefs. 'You think your prayers can save you?

Brahma granted me insurmountable prowess because of my allegiance to him. Praying to a heap of sand will not change your fate.'

Undeterred, Kamarupeshwara resumed chanting: '*Om Namah Shivaya*.'

Infuriated by the king's insolence, Bhimasura's anger intensified. 'Who is this god you pray to so ardently? You are blinded by your belief. Your god cannot stop me. I am invincible!'

Still, there was no reaction from Kamarupeshwara, who remained immersed in his prayers. Bhimasura, reaching the precipice of his patience, swung his sword towards the *lingam* and the king's head in one fell swoop.

As Bhimasura's sword grazed the sand-formed *lingam*, the ground trembled beneath his feet. In an instant, a majestic figure emerged from the sacred structure, and the atmosphere crackled with the arrival of an otherworldly being. Mahadeva materialized, in a spellbinding display of tour de force.

His appearance was nothing short of majestic. His third eye blazed open, radiating a fiery intensity, while His wild matted locks hung freely, reminiscent of a torrential waterfall of vitality. A crescent moon adorned His forehead, and His neck bore the weight of a serpent, representative of His unmatched power. His body, smeared with ash, displayed His asceticism and His transcendence beyond worldly attachments.

'Bhimasura! I have observed your reign of terror upon both the celestial and terrestrial realms. Your attempt to slay a devout supplicant of mine marks the culmination of your transgressions. Prepare yourself, for this shall be your ultimate confrontation.'

Bhimasura, arrogant in his defiance, laughed at Mahadeva's proclamation, igniting the commencement of a mighty battle. Mahadeva displayed a form that embodied a placid equilibrium – a serene yet formidable presence.

Their clash unfolded like a tempestuous storm, raging with unrelenting fury and cataclysmic force. With each strike, Mahadeva's form flickered in and out of view, evoking raw power and unsurpassable might. The unfolding spectacle left the onlookers oscillating between awe and fear.

'Why do You not end this battle instantly? Why prolong the inevitable?' questioned Narada Muni, one of the spectators, articulating the collective sentiment of the mortal and supernatural audiences alike. In response, Mahadeva emitted a mighty roar, His potent third eye releasing a torrent of fire, consuming Bhimasura and everything in its path.

As the flames subsided, the scorched land transformed astoundingly into a lush landscape adorned with medicinal plants. Bhimasura, who had terrorized multiple jurisdictions, was vanquished. Grateful for Mahadeva's timely intervention, the bystanders of the unfathomable display assembled to express their gratitude and request that He permanently reside in the spot where the battle had taken place.

With a compassionate smile, Mahadeva looked upon them and said, 'Your request shall be granted. I shall reside permanently in this sacred spot where the battle has transpired.' His form shifted into the embodiment of victory, the *lingam* known as Bhimshankar - the one who slayed Bhimasura. As the divine presence settled, Mahadeva, in the form of Bhimshankar, stood as a monument to the triumph of righteousness, and the unwavering love and protection offered to His devotees.

*In an alternative origin tale of the Bhimashankar jyotirlinga*, the saga unfolded with the *asura* Tripurasura, who, through intense penance, sought to please Lord Shiva. Pleased with his untiring practice, Mahadeva granted Tripurasura the boon of immortality, accompanied by the crucial condition that the boon should be utilized for virtuous deeds.

However, Tripurasura, swayed by his malevolent inclinations, chose to defy Lord Shiva. He unleashed torment upon the worlds, wreaking havoc and suffering.

In response to Tripurasura's malicious actions that inflicted devastation, Mahadeva and Parvati united their esoteric forms into a singular, awe-inspiring manifestation known as *ardha-narya-nateshwara*. This combined form represents the serene blending of Lord Shiva's masculine energy (Narayana) and Goddess Parvati's feminine energy (Narayani).

As *ardha-narya-nateshwara*, Lord Shiva and Goddess Parvati appeared as a magnificent androgynous being, symbolizing the inseparable union of masculine and feminine energies in the cosmos. The right half of the form embodies Lord Shiva's characteristics, including the sacred ash smeared on the skin, the crescent moon on the forehead and the serpentine adornments. On the left side, the graceful and nurturing attributes of Goddess Parvati are evident, with flowing hair, delicate ornaments and an aura of maternal tenderness.

This unique form of *ardha-narya-nateshwara* not only demonstrated the supreme couple's unity but also served as a potent force against the malevolent Tripurasura. Together, Lord Shiva and Goddess Parvati embarked on a punitive expedition to confront and vanquish the *asura*, bringing an end to his tyrannical reign.

The sacred union of *ardha-narya-nateshwara* epitomized the harmony of the cosmos and the interplay of coupling forces. Through this manifestation, Lord Shiva and Goddess Parvati exemplified the eternal dance of creation, preservation and destruction that sustains the Universe.

The battle that ensued between the deific and the *asura* was immense, with Mahadeva ultimately emerging victorious over Tripurasura's nefarious forces. Although Tripurasura proved no match for the Destroyer, the arduous conflict left Mahadeva fatigued. Seeking respite, Mahadeva descended to the Sahyadri hills and settled on the slopes.

As Mahadeva rested on the hills, the sweat that poured from His sacred form flowed copiously down the inclines, giving birth to the River Bhima. Witnessing this phenomenon, the *deva*s beseeched Mahadeva to eternally bless the sacred spot with His ever-glowing presence. To grant their request, Mahadeva chose to manifest Himself as the Bhimashankar *jyotirlinga*.

Tripurasura's two wives, Dakini and Shakini, heartbroken by the demise of their husband, prayed earnestly to Mahadeva. Touched by their love, He granted the grieving wives the boon of immortality, thus earning the appellation '*Dakinyam Bhimashankara*'.

*In some versions of this story, King Kamarupeshwara is known as* King Sudakshina.

While the Bhimashankar *jyotirlinga* is widely believed to be located in Maharashtra, 'Dakini' and the region of Kamarupa fall squarely in the Guwahati region of Assam today. Incidentally, while not very well known, there is a Bhimashankar *linga* there, which some believe to be the Bhimashankar *jyotirlinga* of this story.

Bhimashankar is located in the Pune district of Maharashtra.

It is the sixth *jyotirlinga*.

# VISHWESHWAR

## Land of Ardhanarishwara and Eternal Salvation

*Sananda-mananda-vane vasantam*
*Ananda-kandam hata-papa-vrindam*
*Varanasi-natha-manatha-natham*
*Shri-vishwanatham sharanam prapadye*

He, who is the foundation of bliss
Who lives with pleasure in the forest of delight
Who extinguishes all cumulative sins
Who is the Lord of all those who are alone
In Vishwanath
The Lord of Varanasi city
I seek refuge.

In the tapestry of Creation, from the primordial void emerged the Supreme Being, Shiva, swathed in the commingling of darkness and light. Within the boundless expanse of this superior essence, a desire took root – an impulse to manifest divergently as male and female, into the imposing *ardhanarishwara*, the union of Shiva and Shakti.

*Ardhanarishwara*, the ideal embodiment of both Shiva and Shakti in a singular form, radiated an ethereal aura that transcended the elements. Their form was a glorious fusion of the masculine and feminine aspects, symbolizing the indivisibility and interconnectedness of sacrosanct energies. They shaped an elysian province where abundance flowed boundlessly – a testament to the perfect equilibrium of male and female energies.

Within this hallowed abode, Lord Vishnu immersed himself in ceaseless prayers. His devotional fervour manifested as a symphony of universal vibrations, precipitating streams and rivers that meandered through the paradisiacal landscape. Among these sacred waters, Manikarnika, also known as Panchakoshi, emerged pure and untouched.

At the will of Lord Shiva, Brahma, born from a blossoming lotus connected to Vishnu's navel, embarked on the creation of the known world. Guided by the watchful oversight of Mahadeva, Brahma sculpted the cosmos. Yet, a distinct portion of this creation, safeguarded by Mahadeva's trident, remained apart as an ethereal space where Vishnu rested after his battles – Manikarnika.

Contemplating the accessibility of this sacred land to devotees, Mahadeva tenderly set it down on earth in the sacred city of Kashi. Transforming into the Avimukta Vishweshwar *lingam*, Mahadeva became the accessible conduit for seekers on their journey to *moksha*.

Munificently, Mahadeva avowed, 'Kashi shall be the sacred place on earth where seekers, on their quest for *moksha*, shall find the sanctum of knowledge, self-exploration, and prayer, a haven where those yearning for *moksha* shall achieve it.'

Thus, Kashi transformed into the earthly abode of salvation, a testimony to the foresight and benevolence of Mahadeva, where the devout find refuge and seekers embark on the transformative journey towards union with the Supreme Being. As Brahma's Day draws to a close and *pralaya* looms on the horizon, Mahadeva orchestrates a critical intervention, with a firm commitment to preserving the sanctity of the land.

To safeguard the sacrosanct land of Kashi during catastrophic cycles, Mahadeva descends from His glacial dwelling to the mortal plane. Cloaked in the etheric vibrations that define His quintessence, Mahadeva wields His *trishul*, the emblem of His omnipotent power. As the all-consuming forces of *pralaya* threaten to engulf everything, Mahadeva positions Himself as the guardian of this sacred area, using His *trishul* to dispense a protective shield and create a sanctuary that shields Panchakoshi from annihilation.

In this act of safeguarding Panchakoshi, Mahadeva stands as the ultimate protector, bridging the otherworldly and mortal planes. His presence ensures that the spiritual haven remains untouched during the cyclical rhythms of creation and destruction, allowing its divinity to endure even in the face of the dissolution of transient worlds.

Mahadeva's intervention has become an act of His universal responsibility and His boundless compassion for those who seek refuge in the holy city.

*The* Skanda Purana *unfolds another narrative of the origin of* Kashi and Kashi Vishwanath.

Once, the renowned Sage Agastya sought clarification from Kartikeya, 'Tell me, O Lord, how did the holy land of Mahadeva, Kashi, come into being? How is it that this land has the unique ability to guide any person who worships Him here to attain *moksha*?'

In response to the sage's inquiry, Kartikeya replied, 'Sage Agastya, my revered mother, Parvati, posed a question to Him, curious about the origin of this preferred parcel of land on earth too. My father recounted to her what I will now relay to you:

'Aeons ago, during the time of the great deluge, everything was submerged in the ocean of darkness, and nothing existed, except Lord Brahma, who is the embodiment of Truth itself. Brahma was omnipresent and omniscient. He was immeasurable and unattainable, and yet, at the same time, he was the one and only expressible Truth. Initially formless, from Infinity, he created a form for himself through his own will. It was in this form that I was created too. From my form, I created Prakriti. It was then that Shiva, Parvati and I manifested at his will.

'It was still the time of deluge, but Shiva did not and could not forsake this holy piece of land that came to be known as Kashi. He lovingly named it '*ananda-vana*' or 'forest of happiness'. As Mahadeva and Parvati looked at their domain of joy, Lord Vishnu actualized and Mahadeva named him Purushottam. Lord Vishnu then created a reservoir with his *Sudharshana Chakra* and filled it to the brim with his perspiration as he continued his austere penance. This *kund* (tank) came to be known as Chakrapushkarini Teerth.

'Mahadeva, with Parvati beside Him, appeared before Lord Vishnu and blessed him abundantly, declaring that the place would be henceforth referred to as Manikarnika [*mani* meaning diamond/precious stone and *karnika* meaning ear] because Mahadeva had once lost His bejewelled diamond earring at that very spot. Vishnu, bowing to Shiva deferentially, enunciated, "Please grace this land with Your blessings of eternal presence. Let anyone who wants to find their way to Your feet attain *moksha* at this very spot. Let this land be named after Your infinite presence. Let this holy land be known as Kashi henceforth."

'Vishnu continued, "This land has lit up with an ethereal light as a result of Your presence. Such light with such radiance cannot be witnessed anywhere else. Hence, this *kshetra* must be referred to as Kashi or the City of Lights."

'Agreeing with the words of the Preserver, Mahadeva affirmed, "This is the land that is most dear to me. I, who have not let this piece of land submerge into the ocean of darkness during the great deluge, shall remain vigilant to prevent any untoward events from occurring here in the time to come. Nothing shall transpire against my wishes or without my consent in this land. Any being who wishes to attain *moksha* may proceed to Kashi and take the name of the Lord with a pure heart." Thus, Mahadeva adorned Kashi with His eternal presence in the form of the Kashi Vishwanath *jyotirlinga*.'

A broad belief suggests that it was the very moment when time commenced its eternal journey that Mahadeva and Parvati stood together as one form. It marks the beginning of the cosmic clock, a timeless union captured in the mystical embrace of Kashi.

The place where the rivers Varana and Asi join the Ganga is called Varanasi, in Uttar Pradesh.

A legend goes that as a tribe called Kasha used to reside in the area, the city came to be known as Kashi.

Kashi Vishwanath is located in Varanasi, Uttar Pradesh.

It is the seventh *jyotirlinga*.

# TRAYAMBAKESHWAR

## The Sin of *Gau-Hatya*

*Sahyadri-sheershe vimale vasantam*
*Godavari-teera-pavitra-deshe*
*Yad-darshanat-patakamashu nasham*
*Prayati tam trayambaka-meesha-meede*

He, who resides on the pure peaks of the Sahyadris
On the hallowed banks of the River Godavari
On seeing whom all sins are destroyed
On that Lord Trayambakeshwar
I meditate.

Rishi Gautama, one of the *saptarishis*, was widely renowned across Bharatavarsha. Known for his intensive spiritual practices and extensive knowledge of scriptures, he was a luminary. His dedication to wisdom and mastery of sacred texts elevated him to a revered position. Gautama's life was dedicated to unravelling the mysteries of existence, earning him a reputation as a sage with unparalleled insight. He was married to the beautiful Ahalya, a creation of Lord Brahma himself.

Rishi Gautama used to travel from place to place all over the land, setting up *ashrams* to teach the masses about ancient literature and scriptures. After he established the *ashrams*, and saw the surrounding lands of the villagers turning fertile, he would move on to another place to lay down the roots of abundance and knowledge there.

On one such expedition of his, Rishi Gautama came across a vast area of land that was terribly drought-stricken. As he walked around in disbelief, sorrow enveloped him. The countryside had altered into a desolate wasteland, devoid of all vibrant life. The verdant fields, previously lush with the promise of plenitude, were now barren expanses stretching as far as the eye could see. No amount of ploughing or fertilizing could resurrect the land to its former richness and bounty.

The barren landscape was a stark contrast to Rishi Gautama's expectations – a shocking and disheartening revelation. Not a patch of fresh grass could be found for the cattle and sheep, the lifeblood of a flourishing village, to graze upon. As Rishi Gautama journeyed on, he encountered deep cracks in the earth, reminiscent of a parched desert. The despair on his face mirrored the bleakness that surrounded him. The solemnity of the situation weighed heavily on his heart, prompting an immediate resolve to alleviate the suffering of the distressed villagers.

In the distance, Rishi Gautama spotted a cluster of huts, but the anticipated sounds of civilization's usual chorus of discordant noises – children's laughter, mothers cautioning their little ones, the banter of farmers tending to their fields – had been replaced by an eerie silence.

He delved deeper into the situation by enquiring in nearby villages. Weary and desperate, the villagers approached him with gratitude for his arrival. 'O Rishi Gautama! We are thankful for your presence. We have no water, and it has not rained for so many years that we have lost count. We are unable to grow crops, and finding water for our basic needs has become a challenge. Please help us, great *rishi*.'

As the villagers poured out their woes, Rishi Gautama felt a surge of pain. The plight of the disconsolate villagers compelled him to find an immediate solution and restore life to the parched land.

In response to his earnest prayers, the atmosphere underwent a remarkable transformation. A subtle shift was evident, as if nature itself paused to listen. Like a divine decree, Varuna, the God of Rain, materialized in a cluster of clouds, their billowing forms pregnant with the promise of relief. These clouds, tinged with hues of grey and white, unfurled across the sky like a majestic tapestry, casting shadows that swirled across the desiccated earth below.

'O revered sage, why have you summoned me here?' Varuna inquired.

Gautama, bowing low, respectfully appealed to the deity, 'Respected Lord, let there be rain on this land to lend some respite to its residents.'

Varuna, gazing helplessly at the remnants of the village, addressed the sage, 'Rishi Gautama, I cannot grant what you seek. Rain did not grace this area because the *devas* did not will it so. I cannot now go against their wishes. Please ask something else of me.'

Undeterred, Gautama persisted, 'Varuna, as the God of Water and Rain, there must be something you can do to aid these dry lands and thirsty people.'

After a moment of contemplation, Varuna replied, 'Gautama, while my hands may be tied, there is still something you can do. Pray to Mahadeva for relief from this unfortunate situation. Only He can help you now. Whatever He directs me to do, I shall do so willingly and without a second thought.'

Following Varuna's counsel, Gautama redirected his prayers towards Mahadeva. The Omniscient, the Lord of the Universe, chose to acknowledge the sincere plea.

As Mahadeva appeared before them, both deity and sage bowed reverentially. 'Mahadeva,' Varuna greeted him, 'your presence brings hope to these parched lands.' Mahadeva nodded in acknowledgement, His gaze sweeping over the barren landscape with solemn understanding.

'Tell me of the plight of this land,' He urged, His voice a gentle yet commanding presence amid the desolation.

Varuna stepped forward, his expression grave as he explained the dire circumstances. 'O Mahadeva,' he began, 'for years, this land has known only drought and despair. The rivers have run dry, and the fields lay fallow.'

Mahadeva's brow furrowed in empathy as He absorbed the weight of Varuna's words. 'We must act swiftly,' He declared. 'Gautama, under Varuna's guidance, you shall dig a pit in the earth to receive the blessings of rejuvenation.'

Gautama nodded solemnly. 'As you command, Mahadeva,' he vowed, his voice steady with purpose.

'Mahadeva, grant us your guidance and blessings to heal this land, to let the waters flow once more and bring life back to these arid plains,' Varuna continued.

Mahadeva's expression softened as He placed a reassuring hand on Varuna's shoulder. 'Fear not,' He said,

His voice a soothing balm. 'With your efforts and my guidance, this land shall flourish once more.'

With the pit finally formed, Varuna's voice carried across the stillness. 'Gautama,' he intoned, 'the time has come to receive the divine waters that shall revive this barren soil.'

Gautama nodded in agreement. 'Indeed, Varuna,' he replied, 'with Mahadeva's blessings, we shall bring life back to this arid land.'

Mahadeva, His presence exuding tranquil wisdom, spoke: 'Your devotion moves me, Gautama. Under Varuna's guidance, you shall be the harbinger of change for this land. Proceed with faith, for your actions shall herald a new era of abundance and vitality.'

Varuna, drawing power from Mahadeva's abundance, then directed the flow of the pure and pristine waters into the pit that Gautama had dug. As the life-giving liquid filled the reservoir, Varuna bestowed his blessings upon it. He spoke, 'This pond of water shall never dry up. It shall have a never-ending supply to quench the needs of the villagers. This body of blessed water shall be named after you, O Compassionate One.'

As the heavenly waters cascaded into the pit, Varuna addressed Him, 'O Mahadeva, Lord of the Universe, Your arrival blesses this scorched land. The waters flow under Your nurturing guidance, and the very earth responds to Your benevolence.'

Acknowledging Varuna's words, Mahadeva turned His gaze towards the devoted sage, saying, 'Gautama, the plight of these villagers and your compassion for them has touched my heart.

'Let this act be a testament to the harmony between the esoteric and earthly realms. Varuna, bless this reservoir with the essence of abundance, and let it be a source of sustenance for generations to come.'

Varuna, following Mahadeva's directive, channelled his quintessence into the water, infusing it with blessings that transcended the temporal constraints of nature. He proclaimed, 'May this pond, named after the compassionate sage Gautama, become a symbol of everlasting grace. Its waters shall quench the thirst of both the land and its inhabitants, ensuring prosperity and abundance.'

In a matter of months, the expanse surrounding the source of water underwent a miraculous transformation. A verdant tapestry of life unfolded as various plants and trees began to flourish in vibrant clusters. The fields once again became fertile, rendering them suitable for cultivation. The rejuvenation extended its benevolent touch to the neighbouring villages, allowing the villagers to plough their fields and harvest an abundance of crops. The blessed land now generously provided everything the people could have ever desired.

Those who had abandoned the region due to the prolonged drought returned to witness the newfound prosperity. Sages, who had sought refuge elsewhere during the times of hardship, came back to the now-thriving land. Even the birds and animals, which had migrated in search of sustenance, returned to find abundant food and shelter in this revitalized sanctuary. The collective intervention orchestrated by Mahadeva and Varuna had not only resuscitated the land but had also rekindled the essence of life and vitality in the hearts of all those who called it home.

Gautama built an *ashram* and decided to reside by the village blessed by Mahadeva.

Every day, his disciples embarked on a journey to the sacred pond to procure water for their daily rituals and prayers. However, they encountered an unexpected hurdle – the wives of the returning sages, seated by the pond, sternly denied the disciples access to the water.

'Wait till we finish our work here first,' they instructed the disciples, turning a deaf ear to their implorations.

Frustrated and empty-handed, the disciples of Gautama returned to the *ashram*.

They shared their grievances with Rishi Gautama. It was collectively decided that his wife, Ahalya, would undertake the responsibility of fetching water from the sacred pond for the daily rituals, so as to not inconvenience the wives of the sages, and ensure the smooth and timely performance of the *ashram* duties.

As dawn broke each day, Ahalya set out on her journey to the pond.

On a serene day, as Ahalya made her way to the pond, she could not help but notice its pristine waters shimmering with an otherworldly serenity. The gentle breeze carried a delicate scent, and the foliage overhead whispered softly in the tranquil air. With a brass vessel in hand, Ahalya approached the pond, intending to draw water for the *ashram*'s rituals. However, her path was unexpectedly blocked by the wives of the sages, who greeted her with unwarranted hostility. Their disdainful words echoed through the air, rebuking Ahalya and casting doubt on her very presence. With nefarious superiority, they wielded their influence to deny Ahalya access to the water from the pond.

Amid the distressing situation, the sages' wives exacerbated tensions by spreading malicious rumours about Ahalya and poisoning their husbands' minds against her. Their hidden jealousy of Rishi Gautama's spiritual prowess and accomplishments fuelled their resentment, perceiving his rising prominence as a threat to their own status and influence. This envy drove them to undermine Gautama and attempt to drive him away from the sacred land.

Seeing an opportunity to tarnish Gautama's reputation, the sages and their wives orchestrated a conflict involving Ahalya at the pond, hoping to discredit Gautama and his *ashram*. The sages and their wives, acting as agents of discord, not only denied Ahalya access to the water but also aggravated the situation with harsh words and slander.

Their actions were part of a calculated scheme to invoke Lord Ganesha, believing that by filling their prayers with grievances against Gautama, they could compel divine intervention to remove him.

Lord Ganesha regarded the sages with solemn eyes. 'Sages,' he began, his voice carrying a premonition, 'you fail to see the truth amid the shadows of jealousy. It is through Rishi Gautama's dedication that this land thrives once more. Yet, you seek to cast him aside, blind to the consequences of your actions.'

One of the sages, his brows furrowed in defiance, retorted, 'Lord Ganesha, we act out of concern for the sanctity of this land. Gautama's influence threatens to overshadow our own. We cannot allow him to remain.'

Ganesha sighed, his gaze shifting from one sage to another. 'Your short-sightedness blinds you to the greater good,' he bemoaned. 'Gautama's virtues far outweigh the threats you perceive. If you continue down this path, you risk losing all that you hold dear.'

But another sage, emboldened by his peers' support, stood firm. 'We will not be swayed by your words, Lord Ganesha,' he declared defiantly. 'Our decision is made.'

Weighed down, Ganesha bowed his head in resignation. 'So be it,' he murmured, his voice tinged with chagrin. 'May destiny guide your path.' And with that, he vanished, leaving the sages to face the consequences of their actions.

After the completion of his daily rituals and austerities, Gautama headed to the fields. It was a bright sunny morning, and he began ploughing the barley field. As he worked, he saw that a cow had come into the field and was grazing there. The cow ate its fill of the crop and then began trampling on what was left of it. Unbeknownst to the sage, it was Ganesha in the form of the cow.

With the intention of protecting the crop, Gautama grabbed a bunch of grass blades and flung it at the cow to shoo it away. Instantly, the cow dropped dead as the grass touched its body.

The sages, who had been hiding behind the wild bushes surrounding the fields, jumped out and began running to the scene. On seeing the body of the dead cow at Gautama's feet, they began yammering at once.

'Look at what Gautama has done!' one sage exclaimed.

'The mighty Gautama has committed *gau-hatya* – he has sinned!' said another.

'Does the Learned One not know that the cow is one of the most revered animals of our faith? A sacred animal in which our gods reside. We pray and worship cows for this very reason. We even refer to them as *gau-mata*.'

'The great *maharishi* has committed a sin!' another sage spoke with sarcasm.

'He must repent or all of us around him will also be doomed to go to *patala loka* with him.'

'We cannot live with a sinner among us.'

'The *devas* will not bestow their blessings on us or accept our humble offerings if we continue to associate ourselves with a cow slaughterer!'

'Repent! Repent! Repent!' they all chanted with mock horror on their faces, as if they had not already planned this very outcome.

Amid the deceptive ploy afoot, the villagers watched in dismay, unable to comprehend the sudden turn of events. Gautama, horrified, found himself isolated and condemned by those he had helped and nurtured. Due to the disdainful accusations by the sages, the villagers, once grateful, now stood divided, torn between loyalty and the apprehension of fury towards their now-thriving territory.

In the midst of all this pandemonium, a stupefied Gautama stared down at his feet in embarrassment. He had not intended for the cow to perish, nor was he able to comprehend how it had happened. He had just wanted to send it away from the fields so that it would not destroy the crops that his disciples and the villagers had worked so hard to cultivate. 'But it is true,' he thought, 'whether I meant to or not, I have committed *gau-hatya* and that is an unforgiveable sin. I must repent for my actions.'

The commotion created by the sages around him made Gautama snap out of his soliloquy. Addressing the angry sages, he said, 'O learned ones, I have committed a sin, as you all have so rightly pointed out to me. I did not intend for my actions to have such an ill-effect, but it has occurred, nonetheless. Therefore, I shall repent. I wish to do so. Please tell me what I should do to seek forgiveness for my actions. I will oblige gladly. I do not wish to cause more harm to any of you, or to any other living soul for that matter.'

As the sages were already prepared for this outcome, they informed the innocent Gautama, 'First, you must move away from this place so as not to pollute any of us with your actions. You must perform severe austerities for at least a month, and you must also circumambulate the earth thrice, all the while chanting 'I killed *gau-mata*.' They issued these lofty directives with the underlying assumption that Gautama would be unable to fulfil them satisfactorily and return.

'You must also pray to Ganga to appear, so you can bathe in her holy waters, and make and worship a thousand *parthiva lingams* of clay or mud. In doing so, you will have repented for your egregious sin of *gau-hatya*.'

And so, without further preamble or hesitation, Gautama embarked on his journey, guided by unspoken grit to fulfil his destiny, no matter the trials that lay ahead.

Gautama began his penance to atone for his sins. Secluding himself, he endured severe austerities for many days, chanting 'I killed *gau-mata*' as he circled the earth thrice. He intensely prayed to Ganga for purification and painstakingly crafted a thousand clay *lingams*, seeking redemption for his sin of *gau-hatya*.

Mahadeva was very pleased with Rishi Gautama's pure intentions and endeavoured to explain to the unsuspecting *rishi* the cunning schemes orchestrated by the sages.

Mahadeva said, 'Gautama, I am very pleased with your submission to me.'

Gautama fell at the Lord's feet immediately and begged for forgiveness for his actions. 'O Lord of the Universe, unknowingly, I have committed a grave sin.' His head stooped in guilt and shame. 'Wash away the sins I have committed, I beseech you.'

Mahadeva continued, 'Gautama, I would forgive you wholeheartedly, if there was anything to forgive. Reality differs from what meets the eye. You have not committed any sin whatsoever. This was all the doing of those sages who were jealous of you and, of course, my mischievous son Ganesha, who was influenced by the entreating prayers of the sages. The cow that died was in fact Ganesha in disguise. You, in fact, did not kill any being!'

Yet, Gautama refused to be pacified. He said, 'O Mahadeva, there can be no greater privilege for me than that of Your appearance before me and blessing me. While I understand what You are telling me, the truth is that, irrespective of who was disguised as a cow, my actions led to its death. Please allow Ganga to appear in this spot so that I can bathe in her holy waters and wash away my sin.'

Mahadeva tried to talk some sense into the venerated *rishi* who stood modestly before Him.

'I need not wash away any of your sins because there are none! As for those sages, who so wrongly drove you away from the land that flourished as a result of your commitment and perseverance, they are another matter. Nothing can absolve them of their devious machinations and treacherous actions. They do not even feel any remorse for it, so blinded are they by the envy that rules their heart.'

Gautama, kind-hearted as he was, replied reverentially, 'But it was because of their wily actions that I have the rare fortune of standing before You and basking in Your supreme glory, my Lord. I must, hence, be thankful to those sages whose schemes and designs have blessed me with Your serendipitous audience.'

Mahadeva, recognizing the innate goodness of the *saptarishi*, said, 'Ask me for anything, gracious Gautama. It shall be granted to you.'

Gautama, after some thought said, 'Mahadeva, please allow me to bathe in the holy waters of Ganga Devi. I will then be rid of the sins I have committed because of my being but human.' And so Mahadeva instructed Ganga to manifest herself. Gautama then bathed in her holy waters and was blessed by Him.

Gautama then said, 'Mahadeva, if I may ask of You one more thing?' He bowed down to his Lord and then looked up at Him with concern in his eyes. 'My Lord,' he continued, 'I do understand that the actions of the sages and their jealousy are unbecoming of them, but they too are but human. It is only natural for *manavas* to feel envy, anger and hatred. Please do not subject them to harsh castigations. Please forgive them, O Mighty One. They are also Your devotees. They may have erred, but even they must be given the opportunity to wash their sins away in the holy waters of Ganga Devi.'

Mahadeva granted Rishi Gautama this request too, saying, 'Gautama, in such a situation I might not have been as forgiving as you have been. You are truly a blessed and evolved soul. You have a deep understanding of human nature and unconditional compassion for all those around you, even those who have so clearly wronged you. Your goodness shall forever be remembered, and it is only for you that I am forgiving those sages and absolving them of their wrongdoing.'

Saying thus, Mahadeva forgave the sages who had tricked and wronged Rishi Gautama.

The sages, having bathed in the waters of Ganga Devi, stood before Mahadeva and Rishi Gautama, now ashamed of their actions. They first begged Mahadeva for forgiveness, to which He said, 'Rise, O sages. Always remember, I would not have been inclined to condone your actions had it not been for Rishi Gautama.'

The sages, having heard that the very man against whom they had fostered hatred and jealousy for so long – the pious man whom they had so wrongly driven out of his own *ashram* – had championed their cause so lovingly before the Lord of Lords, stood speechless. Filled with embarrassment and remorse, they fell at Rishi Gautama's feet.

'Forgive us, Rishi Gautama!' they cried. 'We never stopped to think of all the good you have done for us and the region.'

Gautama, more embarrassed than happy with the attention and the repentant words, conveyed to the sages, 'There is nothing for me to forgive, O sages. We are all human. We all have flaws. And when Mahadeva Himself has been kind enough to pardon you all, who am I to say otherwise?'

Ganga wanted to return to Kailasha with Mahadeva but He told her to remain on earth so that others may also have a chance to wash away their sins by bathing in her purifying waters: 'Dearest Ganga, every *manava* must be given the opportunity to repent, and you, my dear, shall provide them with it, so they may rectify their ways and become better.'

Ganga acceded to this direction of Mahadeva on the condition that she would not be separated from Him or Goddess Parvati. She wanted them to remain on earth with her and so Mahadeva manifested Himself as the

Trayambakeshwar *jyotirlinga*, and Ganga came to be known as 'Gautami Ganga'.

*There are several stories surrounding the origin of the* Trayambakeshwar *jyotirlinga*.

One version of the story suggests that it was not Ganesha disguised as a cow who was killed but Goddess Parvati's close friend Jaya.

*Another story of the origin of Trayambakeshwar can be traced* to the *Pada Purana*. According to this rendition, during the famous episode of the *samudra manthan* or the churning of the Ocean of Milk by the *devas* and the *asuras* to obtain the nectar of immortality contained in the *amritakumbha*, the *devas* obtained the *amritakumbha* by fooling the *asuras* with the help of Lord Vishnu in the guise of the beautiful maiden, Mohini.

When the *asuras* became aware that they were the victims of deceit, they began to fight for the *amritakumbha*. During this battle, which the *asuras* eventually lost, four drops of nectar fell on the earth at four sacred sites – Haridwar, Prayag, Ujjain and Trayambakeshwar – and this led to Trayambakeshwar (or Trimbakeshwar) becoming one of the holiest spots on earth. Befittingly, the world-famous Kumbha Mela is held at these four places once every twelve years.

The Ganga that came down to allow Rishi Gautama to wash away his sins is today referred to as the River Godavari (Dakshina Ganga or Godavari Ganga). The pond that never dries up is referred to as Kushavarta.

The Trimbakeshwar Temple is situated a little distance away from the city of Nashik, near the Brahmagiri Hills in Maharashtra.

It is the eighth *jyotirlinga*.

# BAIDYANATH

## Devotion of the Demon King

*Purvottare prajjwalika-nidhane*
*Sada vasantam girija-sametam*
*Surasura-radhita-pada-padmam*
*Shri-vaidyanatham tamaham namami*

He, who resides with Girija (Parvati)
In the funerary grounds in the north-east
He, whose lotus feet are venerated
By all *asuras* and *devas*
I bow to that Vaidyanath.

Ravana. Demon king. Ruler of Lanka. Renowned for having ten heads instead of the usual one and twenty arms instead of the usual two. Well-known and ardent devotee of Lord Shiva. His intellectual prowess and physical acumen ensured he remained unvanquished as Lanka's overlord.

Half-brahmin, half-demon, he was the son of Vishravas, who was the grandson of Pulastya, one of the ten mind-born sons of Brahma. His mother, Kaikasi, was born of the *asura* clan, thus allowing him to draw legitimacy as the ruler of the *asura* world.

Despite his infamous transgressions as the demon king of Lanka, he was fuelled by unyielding fealty to Mahadeva. With the intense hope of getting at least a glimpse of his beloved God, he continued his spiritual practices with fervour. Despite the lack of acknowledgement from above or an eagerly sought-after appearance, Ravana clung to his determination, refusing to succumb to despair. Time passed, and as the years unfolded, the tenacious ruler held on to the belief that his Lord would eventually respond to his devoted prayers. Ravana's ceaseless credence during such prolonged expectation reflected his commitment to his spiritual pursuits.

Over time, beginning to feel disheartened by the complete absence of any acknowledgement from his

Lord, an increasing restlessness began to take hold of him. He started to yearn for even the briefest glimpse of Mahadeva. In an exigent attempt to please his Lord, Ravana meticulously dug a deep pit on the slopes of the Himavan mountains. Filling it with timber, he began kindling a fire with great care. Directing his words to Mahadeva, he declared, 'My Lord! I have devoted numerous years of my life in rigorous penance to gain Your favour, hoping that You would bless these wretched eyes of mine with Your presence. Yet, You have not deemed me worthy enough. I refuse to live a life untouched by Your grace. I am willing to sacrifice each of my heads to honour You, O Venerable Deity. If You do not come to me, I shall offer myself as a token of unflinching zeal.' With these words, Ravana commenced cutting off his heads one by one, presenting them to Mahadeva.

Ten...

Nine...

Eight...

Seven...

Six...

Five...

Four...

Three...

Two...

Ravana consecrated his heads to the sacred fire, with the utterance of the Lord's name accompanying the severing of each head. 'Har Har Mahadeva!' echoed his roars as the flames embraced each sacrifice. With only one head remaining, Ravana poised his sword to offer his final sacrifice to Mahadeva.

As he raised his sword, ready to sever his remaining head, Mahadeva, moved by the intensity of Ravana's passion, manifested before him. The Lord stood statuesquely, witnessing Ravana's tears of ecstasy as the demon king prostrated before the Lord of the Universe.

'Rise,' Mahadeva spoke placidly. 'Why have you summoned me here?' he inquired of the demon king, finally acknowledging the depth of Ravana's sincerity.

Ravana's heart overflowed with a myriad of emotions as he prostrated himself before Mahadeva. 'O Lord of lords, how I have thirsted for a sight of You. Your fortuitous visage is one to behold!' The realization of the fruition of his arduous penance brought forth a substantial sense of gratitude and awe.

'I am now truly blessed,' Ravana exclaimed, his voice trembling. However, his joy was tempered by the unfulfilled desire lingering in his heart. Ravana longed for Mahadeva to accompany him back to Lanka, believing that the presence of the Lord was indispensable for his reign to be truly spectacular.

'Please come back to Lanka with me, my Lord,' he pleaded. 'I cannot rule without Your guiding light by my side. Please grace my reign with Your presence. I will then be the greatest king to have ever lived, under Your grace and patronage,' Ravana continued, his desperation evident in every word.

Yet, Mahadeva remained silent, His enigmatic gaze fixed upon Ravana. Undeterred, Ravana continued to implore, 'Please, Mahadeva,' as he bowed before his Lord. However, Mahadeva, in His infinite wisdom, refused to accede to Ravana's request.

Instead, He offered a compromise. 'I cannot come with you to Lanka. My place is in Kailasha. I will give you a *lingam*. Carry it with you to Lanka. As the *lingam* is a form of me, it will be as if I am with you. But, mind you, you must not set the *lingam* down anywhere until you reach Lanka, for once you set it down, there is no power in the Universe that will allow you to lift up the idol again. Be aware of your actions,' cautioned Mahadeva.

With these words, Mahadeva disappeared as abruptly as He had appeared, leaving the king of Lanka with the endowed *lingam* and the weight of his fortune on his shoulders.

Ravana stood rooted to the spot with his hands bowed reverentially, as a miraculous transformation unfolded before his eyes. Slowly, the nine heads that he had sacrificed in the name of Mahadeva were restored by the grace of the Lord. Healing kinetics coursed through his veins, weaving together the severed heads seamlessly, each one returning to its rightful place.

An overpowering sense of awe and renewed gratitude enveloped Ravana as he witnessed the miracle. The restored heads served as a tangible testament to the boundless compassion and benevolence of Mahadeva.

With no alternative available, given Mahadeva's refusal to accompany him to Lanka, Ravana lifted the *lingam* from the sacred spot where Mahadeva had stood and commenced his journey to his kingdom of Lanka. As he proceeded, an increasing urge to relieve himself presented a predicament, because he could not place the *lingam* down anywhere along the way.

Observing a cowherd boy walking nearby, Ravana entrusted him with the *lingam*, emphasizing the imperativeness of not setting it down. Seeking a secluded clump of bushes for a brief respite, Ravana left the *lingam* in the cowherd's care. However, the *lingam*'s weight escalated, surpassing the cowherd's capacity. Eventually, succumbing to the burden, the cowherd placed the *lingam* on the ground.

Upon his return, a surge of emotions overwhelmed Ravana. Initially furious at the cowherd's disregard for his instructions, he then sank into despondency, reluctantly accepting the irreversibility of the situation. Recognizing the impossibility of transporting the *lingam* to Lanka, Ravana decided to consecrate it where it had been set down, delineating the establishment of the Baidyanath *jyotirlingam*.

*As Mahadeva assumed the role of a compassionate healer*, tending to and curing Ravana's self-inflicted wounds to win the Lord's favour, Mahadeva earned the epithet 'Baidyanath', a tale recounted in the *Shiva Purana*. However, another version suggests a deeper layer to this narrative.

The bestowal of the *lingam* to Ravana by Mahadeva raised concerns among the *devas* in *swarga loka*. Aware of Ravana's declared intentions to wage war against the *devas*, they feared his invincibility with Mahadeva by his side in Lanka. On his way back with the *lingam*, as the sun began to set, Ravana realized that the hour for his evening prayers was fast approaching. Reluctant to miss it, yet unable to perform his prayers with the *lingam* in hand, he faced a dilemma.

In this critical moment, Lord Vishnu appeared before Ravana in the guise of a shepherd. Sensing Ravana's predicament, he volunteered to hold the *lingam* for Ravana to perform his evening oblations to Mahadeva. However, Vishnu, disguised as the shepherd, cautioned Ravana not to prolong his prayers, as he would leave if Ravana was delayed.

Unaware of the shepherd's true identity, Ravana entrusted the *lingam* to him and proceeded for his ablutions. Seizing the opportunity, Vishnu set down the *lingam* and vanished. Upon Ravana's return, he discovered the *lingam* set down, realizing that, as per Mahadeva's warning, once placed, it could not be moved again. Resigned to his fate, Ravana accepted that Mahadeva would not accompany him back to Lanka.

*In an alternative version of the story, the* devas, *concerned about* Ravana's invincibility with the *lingam*'s extraordinary abilities, gathered and sought help from Varuna. Their intention was to induce an urgent need in Ravana to relieve himself, creating an opportunity to separate him from the *lingam*. In response to their plea, Lord Ganesha manifested before Ravana, offering to hold the *lingam* while he went for his ablutions.

*In yet another rendition of the tale, Lord Vishnu appealed to* Ganga to enter Ravana's stomach as he carried the *lingam* back to Lanka. Meanwhile, Vishnu assumed the guise of a cowherd to take hold of the *lingam* while Ravana attended to his needs in the shrubbery. By strategically placing the *lingam* down, Vishnu thwarted Ravana's plan to transport it to Lanka.

Legend has it that the name 'Baidyanath' was derived from 'Baiju', the name of the cowherd who began worshipping the *lingam* every day.

*In one more rendition of this gripping tale, Narada Muni,* known for his capricious nature, arrived in Lanka to weave another of his impish schemes. Narada Muni requested Ravana to narrate the remarkable encounter between him and Mahadeva. 'You are one of the fortunate few to witness Mahadeva in full glory,' said Narada Muni. 'Share this fated occurrence with me, O King of Lanka, so that I may relive the tale through your words.'

A prideful Ravana began recounting the tale of his communion with the great Mahadeva. He spoke of years of fervent prayers, the sacrificial act of severing his heads, and their subsequent restoration by Mahadeva, along with the bestowment of supreme power and strength. As Ravana approached the climax of his narrative, he conceitedly proclaimed to Narada Muni, 'With the power vested in me by the Lord Himself, I am unstoppable. I will conquer all three worlds, and everyone shall bow before me.'

Narada Muni, usually lively and talkative, fell into an unusual silence. Feigning concern for the unsuspecting *asura* king, he waited for Ravana to take the bait.

'What is the matter, Narada Muni? Is something wrong? Did I say something offensive?'

Narada Muni, seizing the moment, cautioned Ravana with a foreboding tone. 'I am pleased to hear the story of how the Lord blessed you. But, Ravana, beware. Mahadeva is so engrossed in His penance that He might have forgotten the boons He magnanimously granted you. Moreover, losing the *lingam* provided by Mahadeva adds to your predicament. Who will guide you to victory over the three worlds? More crucially, who will help you sustain this triumph without the Lord's guidance?'

Worry creased Ravana's brow. Narada Muni's words had struck a chord, and the thought of Mahadeva's potential forgetfulness during His prolonged penance left the demon king anxious. The cowherd's inadvertent act of setting down the *lingam* had rendered Ravana's god-given strength useless in lifting it once again. Bewildered and seeking a solution, Ravana implored Narada Muni for guidance to secure His power and blessings.

Narada Muni positioned himself as a well-wisher and confidant. He proposed a solution to Ravana's quandary, speaking as if the demon king had approached him with a problem that only he could resolve. Ravana vowed to follow any directive that would please the Lord and safeguard His propitious boons.

The sage, with a serious countenance, advised Ravana, 'You must refresh Mahadeva's memory. This is the only way!' Ravana, entranced by the moment, questioned how he could achieve this.

Narada Muni assured him that for a being of his prowess, the task was not difficult – Ravana needed to lift the great Mount Kailasha, where Mahadeva was deeply engrossed in penance, and gently set it down. This act would not only jog Mahadeva's memory and sense of responsibility towards His humble devotee but also showcase Ravana's unparalleled power to the world.

Caught up in the excitement, Ravana failed to consider the potential repercussions of his actions. He enthusiastically thanked Narada Muni for bringing to his notice critical matters that had eluded him, and guiding him forward. Without a second thought, he hurriedly left to execute Narada Muni's bidding, eager to profess his gratitude to the Lord through his actions.

Lifting Mount Kailasha effortlessly, Ravana became the unwitting disruptor of Mahadeva's penance. The Lord was abruptly pulled out of His contemplative state. Anger surged through Mahadeva as He thundered, 'Who dares disturb my penance?' Unbeknownst to Ravana, his attempt to express gratitude would, in fact, set in motion the circumstances leading to his eventual downfall.

As the realization dawned upon Mahadeva that Ravana was the cause of the disturbance that had pulled Him out of His penance, His anger intensified. The Lord, irked by Ravana's audacity, expressed His indignation aloud. 'How dare he disturb me, even after I went to him and granted him his wishes?' uttered Mahadeva to no one in particular.

Unaware of the storm brewing in his Lord's mind, Ravana, content with the assumption that Mahadeva would now be made aware of his gratitude and reminded of the bestowed boons, gently set down Mount Kailasha after a few seconds of effortlessly holding the majestic mountain. He walked away, assured that his actions had earned him a most opportune favour.

However, what Ravana failed to take notice of was the chilling prophecy that escaped Mahadeva's lips. Unheard by the departing demon king, Mahadeva's curse echoed across the planes of existence, 'Arrogant *asura*, the one who shall destroy your vanity shall soon be born.' The ominous words hung in the air, foretelling a destiny that would unfold with the passage of time.

The Baidyanath Temple is located in Deogarh, Jharkhand. Deogarh means the *garh*, or 'abode' of the God (where Mahadeva resides).

This temple is unique as it is one of the very few places in India where a *jyotirlinga* and a *shaktipeetha*, a sacred site for the worship of Sati, are found together.

It is the ninth *jyotirlinga*.

# NAGESHWAR

## Parvati and Mahadeva's Clash of Duties

*Yamye sadange nagare-tiramye,*
*Vibhushitangam vividhaischa bhogaih*
*Sadbhakti-mukti-pradameesha-mekam*
*Shri-naganatham sharanam prapadye*

He, who resides in the delightfultown of Sadanga
In the south
He, who is well-adorned
Who bestows all manner of pleasures
Of that Lord Naganatha
The only One who bestows both devotion and liberation
I seek protection.

Daruk, a dreadful *asura*, formed a menacing pair with his wife, Daruka. Both epitomized malevolence, finding immense pleasure in spreading fear throughout their surroundings. Their nefarious activities included the ruthless destruction of homes, the slaughter of innocent animals, and, for sheer amusement, hunting down helpless villagers. The villagers, subjected to the daily horrors inflicted by this wicked couple, endured a life fraught with constant fear for their very existence.

In the face of such unbearable torment, the distressed villagers sought solace and aid from Sage Aursh, who resided nearby. Sage Aursh, also known as Aurva, held a revered lineage, being the son of Urva, who, in turn, was the descendant of the illustrious Bhrigu.

In a chorus of desperate pleas, they poured out their grievances before him.

'O revered *rishi*! The demon Daruk and his wife, the demoness Daruka, have unleashed terror upon us,' they bewailed. 'Our homes are reduced to ashes, and our fields lie ravaged in their wake. These evil beings revel in harassing us and burning down our dwellings without remorse. Our lives are filled with perpetual dread.'

As they prostrated themselves at the feet of Sage Aursh, their voices rose in unison, 'Please save us, venerable *rishi*! You are our sole sanctuary. Only your actualization can stop these demons.'

Sage Aursh, witnessing the anguish of the people, could not tolerate the excruciation inflicted upon them by the demon-couple. The impudence of these cruel beings, thinking they could freely reign and terrorize innocents, ignited an immense anger within the sage. It was time, he thought, to impart a lesson.

Sage Aursh addressed his troubled followers: 'Do not worry, my beloved people. I shall find a solution for your predicament. Please return to your homes, and rest assured that Daruk and Daruka shall never bother any of you again.'

Having previously undertaken rigorous austerities, Aursh possessed the knowledge required to summon the *devas* at his command. With this wisdom, he was ready to call upon them to assist his followers in their struggle against the torment inflicted by the *asuras*.

The *devas*, ageless beings of ethereal beauty, manifested before Sage Aursh in a radiant display; their visages were adorned with luminosity, and each deity exuded an aura of tranquillity and abundance. Their eyes, pools of regality, gazed upon Sage Aursh with a readiness to heed his call.

'Why have you summoned us?' inquired the *devas*, responding to Aursh's prayers.

Sage Aursh determinedly appealed to the *devas*, 'O sentient beings, the demon Daruk and his wife, Daruka, have been terrorizing innocent people, pervading these lands with their pride and ego. This realm is steeped in fear due to the bloodshed caused by this *asura* couple. Please, I beseech you, help the blameless people residing in these areas.'

Responding to the sage's impassioned plea, the *devas* assumed a battle-ready stance to confront the bellicose *asura* couple. The tenacious warriors, armed with their astral arsenal, advanced with commitment to vanquish the source of terror and restore order in the region.

As the battle unfolded, the clash between the immortal *devas* and the mortal *asura* couple was fierce and relentless. Infernal munitions clashed against the demonic forces, and the battlefield shook with the thunderous clash of powers.

The *asura* couple, Daruk and Daruka, soon became cognizant of their diminishing forces and the overwhelming might of the *devas*. Realizing the futility of pursuing this war, they made a strategic retreat, withdrawing from the battlefield to deliberate on their immediate course of action. The pride that had once fuelled their aggression now gave way to pondering how to navigate the challenges posed by the *devas*.

Daruka, a devoted follower of Goddess Parvati, conducted rigorous penance to seek the blessings of the Divine Mother, for with her support, Daruka would be able to sufficiently counteract the attack by the *devas*.

In the sacred presence of Goddess Parvati, Daruka knelt, her sombre earnestness shining as brightly as the heavenly light that surrounded the goddess. Parvati, in her resplendent form embodied grace and compassion; her brilliance radiated, illuminating the sacred space surrounding her.

As Daruka uttered her earnest prayer, Parvati's presence cast a warm and comforting glow. The goddess listened to the plea with a benevolent expression, her eyes reflecting wisdom in their depths.

'Rise, devoted one,' Parvati said, her voice a melodic resonance that encapsulated blissful assurance. 'I shall bestow upon you a boon of unparalleled power. May you be endowed with the strength to face challenges and emerge victorious.'

As the words left Parvati's lips, a gentle yet potent aura enveloped Daruka. An unearthly energy, transformative, surged through her being, infusing her with newfound vigour. In that singular moment, Daruka felt the embrace of the goddess's blessings, knowing she was now chosen and empowered by the Protective Mother.

After receiving this boon, Daruka thoughtfully approached her husband. 'Dear husband, the time has come for us to plan our next steps. I am aware of a secret sanctuary - an unknown island in the vast ocean. This hidden refuge is known only to me, and we can seek solace there until the tides of fate turn in our favour.'

Daruk, in agreement with his wife's prudent suggestion, responded, 'Indeed, my beloved. This secret island serves us perfectly, shielding us from the imminent threats. It also offers us the precious time needed to devise our retaliation against the *devas* who dared to meddle in our lives and sought to end us. Lead the way, dear wife, and take us to the sanctuary with your newly acquired powers.'

Daruka harnessed her elevated abilities to transport herself and Daruk to the clandestine island. This move allowed them respite before the resumption of their ruthless pursuits.

With the passage of time, the *devas*' relentless pursuit waned. Those days were a blissful interlude for the couple, cocooned from the campaigns against them on the mainland. With no inclination to return, the couple embraced a life of contentment, revelling in their halcyon isolation. Some of their accomplices also joined them on the island, seeking refuge to pursue their nefarious ways on the ocean instead of on land.

Their days were now dedicated to a different but similar pursuit – capturing and tormenting any unfortunate beings traversing the seas near their island. The *asuras*, driven by primal instincts, became formidable predators of the vast ocean.

One sunlit day, the sky in golden hues, a fleet of ships sailed near their island. Without hesitation, Daruk and Daruka sprung to capture the fleet, seizing the people onboard as hostages. The captives, now victims of the *asura* couple's ruthless whims, found themselves confined in eerie dungeons on the secluded island. The damp chambers echoed with the sinister traces of the past, remnants of those tortured, killed and possibly devoured by the cruel *asuras*.

Among the captives, a man, Supriya, stood out – a devout follower of Mahadeva, steadfast and true even in the grim confines of his incarceration. Despite the oppressive conditions, Supriya continued his daily worship of Lord Shiva. In the acrid-smelling dungeon that served as his prison, he resourcefully fashioned a *lingam* with whatever materials were available.

'*Om Namah Shivaya!*' was audible within the damp and suffocating walls as Supriya, eyes closed, enraptured, pictured his beloved Lord in his mind's eye. With folded hands, he chanted the names of Mahadeva, finding solace amid the hardships. Witnessing Supriya's firm faith, the other hostages, motivated by his conviction, joined in the worship of Mahadeva.

Days turned into a comforting succession of prayers within the dungeons. In the face of adversity, the prisoners sought refuge in chanting the Lord's name, believing that only He could offer salvation. The *asuras* guarding them, unable to fathom the depth of Supriya's faith, resorted to mockery and stone-throwing. Despite the harassment, Supriya's piety shone as a beacon of inspiration for those around him.

When Daruk discovered Supriya engrossed in his prayers, rage consumed him. 'Who are you worshipping?'

he thundered, demanding an answer. Lost in his unselfish supplication, Supriya remained silent, further infuriating Daruk. The *asura*, seething with anger, raised his weapon with the intent to slay Supriya on the spot.

In that critical moment, a brilliant flash of lightning heralded the timely arrival of Mahadeva. With a mere glance, Mahadeva turned Daruk and the surrounding *asuras* to ashes. The hostages, witnessing this miraculous rescue, rejoiced and bowed down in veneration, expressing gratitude for the Lord's intervention in their dire circumstances.

However, Mahadeva's wrath had not yet subsided. He pursued every *asura* on the island, systematically reducing them all to ashes one by one. The island, once a haven for the malevolent *asura* couple and their legions, now bore witness to the purifying fury of Mahadeva.

Upon learning of her husband's demise at the hands of Mahadeva, Daruka was overcome with heartbreak. Desperate and in anguish, she sought Goddess Parvati's protection. With tearful eyes, she cried out, 'O Mighty Goddess! Your husband, Mahadeva, has slain my husband. Please protect me. You have been my safe haven in times of need. I implore you to shield me from the wrath of Mahadeva.'

Despite Daruka's past sins, Goddess Parvati, recognizing the sincerity of her urgent pledge, could not allow Mahadeva to harm her devotee. Duty-bound to protect her ardent worshipper, Parvati assured, 'Stand behind me, Daruka. I shall shield you.' Daruka bowed at

Parvati's feet and swiftly took cover behind the fierce goddess, knowing that only she could intercede and safeguard her from Mahadeva's impending wrath.

Mahadeva approached with bloodshot eyes, His *trishul* held up menacingly, and thundered, 'Where is Daruka? Where is that vile *asura* woman who has caused nothing but grief to so many of my beloved devotees?' His wild matted locks danced in the air, matching the intensity of His anger. His third eye throbbed on His forehead, poised to unleash its fury and reduce everything in its path to ashes.

A tense standoff unfolded as Parvati positioned herself between her husband and her trembling devotee. Calmly, she addressed Mahadeva: 'O Lord, I cannot in good conscience allow You to kill Daruka.' Her words halted Mahadeva in His tracks. The perplexity on His face was evident, as He had not anticipated this objection from His wife.

Attempting to rationalize His intent, Mahadeva explained, 'She is an *asura* who has tormented and killed so many people. I have to slay her as an act of retribution to protect my devotees, whom she unjustly imprisoned on her island.'

Parvati, with equal conviction, countered, 'Mahadeva, just as those people are Your devotees, and You would go to any extent to protect them, Daruka is mine. She worships me every single day. Therefore, I must protect her from Your vengeance.' The husband and wife found themselves at an impasse, torn between their duties towards their respective devotees.

At that critical juncture, a profound realization dawned upon both Mahadeva and Parvati. They comprehended that their duties, as well as their commitment to safeguarding their respective devotees, had led them to this stalemate.

As they realized the delicate balance between their obligations to their devotees and to each other, Mahadeva and Parvati, with cohesive resolve, transcended their individual forms to become a single, radiant *lingam*. This symbolic metamorphosis signified their unity in purpose and their commitment to shielding their devotees from potential conflict. The *lingam* became a powerful emblem, serving as an impenetrable shield that ensured the protection of devotees, and Mahadeva and Parvati's unity as the *lingam* stood as a testament to their eternal love and universal posterity, and the balance they maintained for the greater good.

*In other versions of the narrative, Daruk receives the boon from* Goddess Parvati, and the place where Lord Shiva defeats the demon is referred to as Darukavanam.

It is not uncommon for different retellings to emphasize various aspects or characters, leading to alternate details and outcomes. In some versions, the role of Goddess Parvati in protecting Daruka might not be highlighted or might be absent altogether. These variations contribute to the richness and flexibility of Hindu mythology, offering different layers of meaning and insights into the complex relationships between deities and devotees. Each rendition adds depth to the narrative, reflecting the diverse cultural and regional influences on the storytelling traditions.

*The story of the Nageshwar* jyotirlinga*'s origin in the* Mahabharata era, involving the Pandavas, adds another layer to the sacredness of this holy site. According to this narrative, in the *dwapara yuga*, during their wanderings in the forest, the Pandavas encountered a remarkable sight: a river brimming with cream and milk. Nestled within the heart of this ethereal river was a *swayambhu lingam*, a self-manifested representation of Lord Shiva.

Drawn to the unknown enigma, Bhima, the mightiest of the Pandavas, retrieved the *swayambhu lingam* from the river. The precise location where Bhima reverently placed the *lingam* is recognized as the sacred site of the Nageshwar *jyotirlinga*.

*In an alternative rendition of this tale, the focus shifts to a group* of devoted dwarves known as the Balakhilyas, who were ardent worshippers of Lord Shiva in Darukavanam. To assess the depth of their spiritual singlemindedness, He assumed the guise of a nude ascetic, adorned only with serpents (*naga*s) around his neck, and arrived in their midst.

The captivating presence of the ascetic stirred the hearts of the dwarves' wives, who were attracted to this bewitching stranger and began to follow him. This unexpected turn of events angered the Balakhilyas, leading them to curse the ascetic, causing him to lose his sanctified form. The repercussions of this culminated with the phallic structure falling to earth.

In response to the ensuing disarray, Lord Brahma and Lord Vishnu pleaded with Mahadeva to intervene and restore equilibrium to the Universe. Mahadeva revealed Himself to the dwarves, who then rushed to seek His blessings. Acknowledging their sacrament, Mahadeva retrieved the phallus structure, vowing to leave His indelible mark on the location in the form of the *jyotirlinga*, a symbol of His eternal presence and grace.

According to popular belief, this temple was located close to Dwaraka, and Lord Krishna himself would visit to worship the *lingam* and perform *rudrabhishekam*, a sacred ritual involving the ceremonial bathing of the Shiva *lingam* with many sacred offerings.

Here, Lord Shiva acquired the name of Nageshwar and Goddess Parvati acquired the name of Nageshwari.

The Nageshwar Temple is in Dwarka, Gujarat. It is the tenth *jyotirlinga*.

# RAMESHWAR

## Saving Sita

*Sutamra-parni-jala-rashi-yoge*
*Nibhadhya setum vishikhaira sankhyaih*
*Sri ramachandrena samarpitam tam*
*Ramesha-rakhyam niyatam smarami*

At the confluence of the River Tamraparni
With the sea
Where a bridge was built by Lord Rama
With countless arrows
I bow faithfully to that Lord of Rameshwar.

Lord Rama, the seventh avatar of Lord Vishnu, incarnated on earth with the noble mission of vanquishing the demon-king Ravana and reinstating *dharma* in Bharatavarsha. A visionary statesman, his character is exemplified by his unshakable commitment to righteousness and the welfare of his subjects.

In the final year of their *vanavas*, the self-effacing and unassuming lives of Rama and Sita were disrupted when the demon-king Ravana abducted Sita and carried her away to Lanka. Rama, driven by his sense of duty and love for Sita, embarked on a perilous journey to rescue her and fulfil his virtuous purpose on earth.

Accompanied by his loyal and supportive brother Lakshmana and the devoted Hanuman, Rama's quest was not just a personal one but the apogee of his indispensable role as an incarnation of Lord Vishnu. The abduction of Sita symbolized the eclipsing of *dharma*, and Rama's mission was to thwart *adharma* and vanquish the arrogant Ravana.

Hanuman, with the extraordinary powers granted to him by various deities during his childhood, played a pivotal role in the search for Sita. His ability to fly across oceans and penetrate enemy territories made him an invaluable asset. Hanuman's deep and unconditional love for Rama, coupled with his exceptional capabilities, entailed him to be the one to find Sita and reassure her of her and Rama's certain reunion.

Upon receiving the crucial information from Hanuman about Sita's captivity in Lanka, Rama comprehended the need for a powerful force to confront Ravana and rescue his beloved wife. In pursuit of this goal, Rama sought an alliance with Sugriva, the *vanara* king of Kishkindha.

Sugriva, while capable and powerful, was facing a challenging situation of his own in Kishkindha. His brother Vali, through unjust means, had taken control of the throne and banished him. The alliance between Rama and Sugriva was based on mutual benefit. Rama pledged to assist Sugriva in reclaiming his kingdom from the tyrannical Vali, and in return, Sugriva committed the support of his indomitable *vanara* army to aid Rama in his quest to rescue Sita. This alliance was not just a strategic military collaboration but also an embodiment of the *dharma* that Rama upheld.

Before embarking on the long and perilous journey to Lanka to seek out Sita and reassure her that every effort was underway to rescue her, Hanuman was entrusted with a token of identification – the ring that Rama wore at all times.

Upon reaching the opulent palace of Ravana, Hanuman meticulously scoured the island kingdom until he discovered Sita's whereabouts in the splendid gardens of Ashokavatika. There, Hanuman stood before Sita, a steadfast emissary bearing Rama's love. With deep reverence, he presented the ring, a tangible manifestation of Rama's eternal commitment and an omen of what was to come.

Hanuman spoke with abiding tenacity, 'O Devi Sita, I am Hanuman, a humble servant of Lord Rama. I bring to you this ring, a symbol of his enduring love and a promise to rescue you from the clutches of Ravana.'

Teary-eyed, Sita accepted the ring. In return, she handed Hanuman a ring of her own, a poignant gesture infused with a message of hope and commitment. 'Tell my husband that my faith in him remains unshaken,' she conveyed with calm strength. 'I await his arrival, for I know he will come to save me. The bond we share transcends this separation.'

Hanuman, deeply moved by Sita's resilience, bowed before her and assured her, 'Mother, your message will reach Lord Rama. He will come, and together, we shall reunite you both. Your faith will guide us in this noble quest.'

As Hanuman left her to return to his lord with the news of his beloved, he saw Sita sitting forlorn beneath a majestic tree bearing witness to the trials and tribulations of her captivity. The dishevelled state of her appearance was unable to diminish her ethereal figure. Her aura, though dimmed by the circumstances, still radiated a stoic fortitude.

The gentle breeze played with strands of her hair, framing her face like a halo. Her attire, once pristine, now bore the marks of strain and hardship. Despite the weariness in her eyes, there was a resilient spirit that emanated from within, a resolve that had withstood the trials of separation.

In the presence of the vast and seemingly insurmountable sea that stretched endlessly before them, Rama and his entourage found themselves standing at the shoreline with the expanse of the ocean separating them from Lanka.

Realizing the daunting challenge that lay ahead, Rama turned to the skies for guidance. He decided to invoke Lord Mahadeva. Gathering the sand from the beach, Rama skilfully moulded a *parthiva lingam*, a symbolic representation of Lord Shiva, and reverently installed it along the shore. Rama sat down to worship Mahadeva, praying for guidance on how to proceed at this crossroads.

As the all-knowing Mahadeva manifested Himself before him, a warm and affectionate smile adorned the countenance of the Supreme Being. Rama, the revered avatar of Vishnu, humbly prostrated himself before Mahadeva, recognizing the enduring presence that had graciously answered his prayers. 'Thank you for heeding my prayers, O Supreme One. I am blessed by the sight of You,' said Rama, expressing his gratitude.

Mahadeva, omniscient and omnipresent, enquired, 'Why have you summoned me here, Dasharatha Nandana? How may I be of service to you?' In response, Rama unfolded the tale of Sita's abduction by the malevolent *asura*-king Ravana, detailing the dire need to cross the vast expanse of water to reach Lanka, where she was being held captive.

Expressing his determination to vanquish Ravana and rescue Sita, Rama implored, 'Please guide us, O Lord! Please show us the way! I am on a mission to slay Ravana and bring my wife Sita safely back home. Please grace me with your blessings, Mahadeva!'

The Supreme Being, with a knowing smile, acknowledged the unfolding destiny. 'So be it,' Mahadeva pronounced, bestowing His assent and sealing Ravana's fate.

To commemorate the intercession, Rama requested that Mahadeva establish Himself at that very spot. The result of this earnest appeal was the manifestation of the Rameshwar *jyotirlinga*, an enduring symbol of Shiva's presence and blessings in the epic journey of Rama.

*In an alternative version of the tale, after successfully slaying* the demon-king Ravana, who was also a brahmin, Rama is burdened by the weight of the sin of *brahmin-hatya*. In his quest for atonement, Rama decides to construct a *lingam*. To fulfil this sacred task, he entrusts Hanuman with the responsibility of bringing stones from the Himalayas.

According to some beliefs, the *lingam* enshrined in the Ramanathaswamy Temple in Rameswaram is considered to be the very idol that Lord Rama crafted with his own hands to seek redemption for the perceived sin of *brahmin-hatya*. This version adds a layer of penance and remorse to Rama's narrative, highlighting the spiritual significance of the Rameswaram *jyotirlinga* in the context of repentance and forgiveness.

*In a parallel narration found in the* Skanda Purana, *the story* unfolds after Rama's victory in the war against Ravana and the rescue of Sita. Following the triumph, Rama graciously crowned Vibhishana, Ravana's righteous younger brother, as the new king of Lanka. Having fulfilled his duty and recognizing that the fourteen-year exile had concluded, Rama, accompanied by Sita, Lakshmana, Hanuman, and his legion of followers, embarked on the journey back to Ayodhya in the *pushpaka vimana*.

During their journey, as the entourage reached the Gandhamadan Mountain, Rama disembarked from the *vimana* and walked around. It was at this moment that a realization struck him – the burden of the sin of *brahmin-hatya* weighed heavily on his conscience.

Tormented by this realization, Rama sought a way to atone for this perceived transgression. To absolve himself of this sin, Rama decided to personally install the Rameswaram *lingam* at the Rameswaram Setu.

As this *jyotirlinga* was installed by the great Lord Rama himself, it is believed that any person who worships this sacrosanct phallic structure shall attain *moksha*.

*In yet another alternative version of this narrative, wise sages of* that era counselled Rama, Lakshmana and Sita to install a *lingam* in Rameswaram as an expression of gratitude to Mahadeva for His blessings during the war and as a means to seek redemption for the perceived sin of *brahmin-hatya.* Acting upon this advice, Rama dispatched Hanuman to Mount Kailasha with the task of bringing back a *lingam* to be established in Rameswaram.

However, due to unforeseen circumstances, Hanuman could not return in time. To ensure the continuity of worship, Sita crafted a makeshift *lingam* from sand for ceremonial purposes. When Hanuman eventually returned with stones from Mount Kailasha, the *lingam* created by Sita was already in place. Although disappointed that he could not present the intended *lingam*, Hanuman's sentiments were assuaged by a declaration by Rama.

In a gesture of understanding and to honour Hanuman's efforts, Rama proclaimed that the *lingam* brought by Hanuman from Mount Kailasha should always be accorded precedence in worship. This tradition endures, with the *lingam* fashioned by Sita being known as 'Ramanathaswamy', and the one brought by Hanuman referred to as 'Vishwalinga'. Thus, the sanctum sanctorum in Rameswaram encapsulates a unique structure of two *lingams*.

The bridge that the *vanara* army built for Lord Rama to cross still exists today, starting from Dhanushkodi in Tamil Nadu and extending to Mannar Island, off the north-western coast of Sri Lanka. It is visible through satellite imaging and is presently submerged underwater. The bridge is measured to be approximately 48 km (30 miles) long.

The Ramanathaswamy Temple has twenty-two wells in its compound. Each well has a special significance. It is believed that a person putting a little water on themselves from each well is equivalent to that person having a cleansing bath. According to the *Skanda Purana*, there are, in fact, sixty-four wells surrounding the temple, but twenty-four of these wells are of the utmost importance. While two of the wells are outside the temple compound, the other twenty-two are inside. It is believed that those who bathe in each of these twenty-two wells will be absolved of all their sins.

The Ramanathaswamy Temple is situated in the coastal town of Rameswaram, Tamil Nadu.

It is the eleventh *jyotirlinga*.

# GRISHNESHWAR

## A Sister's Envy

*Ilapure ramya-vishalake-asmin*
*Samulla-santam cha jagad-varenyam*
*Vande maho-dara-tara-svabhavam*
*Ghrishneshwarakhyam sharanam prapadye*

He, who is seated in Ilapura
He, who is worshipped by the entire Universe
Who is magnanimous by nature
I seek refuge in that Grishneshwar.

Profound devotees of Mahadeva, Sudharma – a descendent sage of Rishi Bharadwaja – one of the formidable *saptarishis*, and his wife, Sudheha, embodied the essence of contentment and joy in simplicity. They lived in a modest *ashram* nestled in the heart of the forest. Unfazed by the allure of riches and opulence, they found solace and fulfillment in the unassuming comforts of their humble hut. The couple revelled in the beauty of the forest, finding joy in the rustling leaves, the melodious songs of the birds, the soft murmur of the nearby stream, and their shared moments of laughter and love. There was but one sorrow that darkened their otherwise tranquil existence. Try as they might, they were unable to have a child to carry on their family name.

Sudheha would occasionally pour out her inner turmoil to Sudharma, seeking solace in their bond. 'Sudharma, my love, I feel a void in our lives. The absence of a child leaves our home incomplete,' she would say, her eyes reflecting her silent longing.

Sudharma, composed and rooted in his faith, would respond reassuringly. 'Fear not, my dear Sudheha,' he would say, his conviction evident, 'our journey is guided by a preordained plan. If it is the will of Mahadeva, He shall bless us with the joy of parenthood in due time. Let us persevere in our prayers and surrender to His wisdom.'

Despite Sudharma's comforting words, Sudheha's yearning lingered in the air. Sudharma's genuine but simplistic approach to her longing sometimes left her feeling unheard as he immersed himself in his rituals, unaware of her silent struggles. In the quiet confines of their home, Sudheha grappled with unspoken emotions as the absence of a child cast a shadow on her happiness. While devoted to her husband, she yearned for the joys of motherhood. Her inner world was an amalgamation of hope, anxiety, fear, urgency, and a periodic reminder of unfulfilled dreams.

In moments of frustration, she tried to convey the depth of her emotions to Sudharma, articulating her needs. 'Motherhood is a blessing,' she would say, her pleas sometimes tinged with anger. 'I do not have all the time in the world, like you, to beget a child,' she once confided, pain reflecting in her eyes.

Seeking remedies from Sudharma, she only received reassurances. His standard reply, 'Do not lose heart, my love. Our time will come,' felt like a distant promise, doing little to ease her ache.

Pleading with her husband to perform rituals or craft potions that might bring forth the cherished child, Sudheha faced a consistent wall of faithful conviction.

Her days revolved around the dream of a healthy child. Wishing for the cries of a baby, Sudheha yearned for motherhood, daydreaming about playing games and singing lullabies. In still moments, she envied other mothers, yearning for the same joy soon.

One day, as Sudheha enjoyed the forest's serenity with the wives of fellow sages, an unforeseen storm brewed. The peaceful atmosphere shattered as a seemingly innocent disagreement escalated into a heated quarrel.

Her companions, caught in anger's grip, directed their antagonism towards Sudheha, aware that their words would inflict deep wounds. Mocking and taunting, they sneered, 'What do you know of motherhood? You are not destined to have a child, let alone a son. Perhaps the Universe is signalling that you are a bad mother. Only He knows what sins you must have committed to remain childless after so many years of marriage.'

The venomous words cut deep, a cruel assault on Sudheha's dreams and desires. Facing their heartless accusations, Sudheha, though wounded, summoned strength. 'You know nothing of my struggles,' she said, 'of the silent battles within. Motherhood is not just a title but a feeling deep within a woman's soul. You may mock me, but you cannot comprehend the pain I carry or the strength it takes to endure such trials. My love for Sudharma, my longing for a child, and sincere pledge to Mahadeva are instilled in every fibre of my being. Do not judge what you cannot understand.'

Yet, her attempts to articulate her emotions fell on deaf ears, drowned by mockery's harsh echoes. As their malicious remarks left harsher wounds, Sudheha sought respite in the forest's embrace. The towering trees, witnesses to her struggles, seemed to sway in empathy, and the gentle breeze whispered a soothing yet melancholic tune.

Returning home, Sudheha poured her heart out to Sudharma. Touched by her sorrow, he resolved to meditate on Mahadeva's form and pray fervently for a child.

Listening to Sudheha's anguished tale, Sudharma comforted her. 'Your pain is mine, your desires etched in my heart. I shall seek Mahadeva's benevolence. Together, we shall endure this storm, and with providence, our prayers shall be answered.' Finding succour in her husband's support, Sudheha embraced the hope that their prayers would bring them the joys of parenthood. For the first time, she felt understood.

Sudharma found a secluded clearing in the heart of the forest. It was bathed in dappled sunlight filtering through the canopy. Here, Sudharma prepared for intense meditation to seek Mahadeva's blessings. Commencing his penance, Sudharma plucked two flowers from the vibrant foliage around him. Holding them gently, he cast them at the feet of his beloved, who stood nearby.

A poignant thought occurred to him: 'If my beloved picks up the flower I throw with my right hand, she will be blessed with a child. But if she picks up the flower I throw with my left hand, she will never be a mother.'

Unaware of her husband's thoughts, Sudheha picked up the flower Sudharma had cast with his left hand. His eyes welled up with tears, contemplating her unknowing choice and sealing her fate.

As he grappled with conveying this to her, Sudheha's voice pierced his veil of thoughts. 'Why are your eyes filled with tears?' she asked. 'What do the flowers represent?'

Sudharma stayed silent. As Sudheha awaited an explanation, anxiety crept into her voice and she implored, 'What is wrong? Tell me!'

Bracing himself, Sudharma cleared his throat and began to explain what had just occurred. 'Beloved, I threw two flowers at your feet. One with my right hand, the other with my left. You picked up the flower from my left hand, ensuring you shall never be a mother.'

Sudheha, eyes filling with pain, crumpled to the forest floor as the consequences sank in. 'Is there nothing we can do?' she wailed. 'What should I do now? Maybe those ladies were right. I must have committed grave sins to be in this predicament.'

Approaching, Sudharma seated himself beside her, and gently took her hand, an unspoken reassurance. 'Sudheha, I understand your pain,' Sudharma began, his voice tender but resolute. 'But understand, without your becoming a mother, I cannot become a father. What is done is done. Devote your life to Mahadeva, pray for release from this cycle of karma. That is the way forward.'

Refusing to surrender to their shattered dream, Sudheha responded, 'Oh, Sudharma, it pains me that I shall never be a mother. But this burden is mine alone. Marry another lady; ensure your name and lineage live on.'

Sudharma rejected the notion vehemently. 'How could you suggest I marry someone else? We took an oath to be faithful. I could never break that vow. I too shall dedicate my life to Mahadeva.'

Moved by Sudharma's love and dedication, Sudheha smiled. Yet, she insisted he be spared her pain and the lineage of the *saptarishi*s, Brahma's descendants, live on. Determined to convince him, she decided to arrange his marriage to someone else.

Sudheha's relationship with her younger sister, Grishna, was marked by a strong bond of sisterhood. With heartfelt concern for Sudharma's happiness, Sudheha approached Grishna and convinced her to marry Sudharma. Under the same guise, she brought her to their *ashram* and despite Grishna's apprehension to the potential emotional complications such marital entanglement may lead to, Sudheha succeeded in persuading her.

'No doubt, Grishna,' she said, 'it will not be a journey devoid of challenges. Yet, I have faith in your strength and understanding. It is a sacrifice, a choice borne out of love for our family. I have come to believe that Sudharma deserves the gift of fatherhood, a legacy to carry forward his family name, one that I am now unable to contribute to. It is a complex decision, but if you consent, I also believe that such an arrangement would bring you much joy and immeasurable blessings to carry on Brahma's lineage.'

Grishna and Sudharma hesitantly agreed to their union, but witnessing Sudheha's unwavering determination, Sudharma could not help but interject one last time, his voice pleading. 'Sudheha,' he said, 'I understand your longing, but let us not rush into this decision hastily. Consider the ramifications for all those involved, including yourself. Our actions today will shape our futures profoundly. Please, let us tread carefully and with full awareness.'

Despite Sudharma's warnings, Sudheha's deep-seated desire for motherhood eclipsed any consideration for future complications. To her longing heart, the means mattered far less than the end, and she was unwilling to heed Sudharma's words of caution. After all, why would she feel badly of her own sister?

Or so she told herself...

Initially, Grishna's arrival brought contentment to Sudheha's heart. The *ashram*, resonant with the prayers and rituals of Sudharma and Sudheha, now also welcomed the gentle presence of Grishna. The trio, bound by their shared devotion to Mahadeva, formed a cohesive unit. Grishna, a tender and thoughtful soul, effortlessly integrated into the *ashram*'s routine, dedicating her days to Mahadeva's worship and affectionately attending to both her husband and sister.

In their spiritual pursuits, Grishna demonstrated her faith by crafting *lingams* out of sand, a symbolic act of worship she faithfully performed daily. Her rituals, including the immersion of one lakh *lingams* in the nearby pond, earned her Mahadeva's abundant blessings over time. Tranquil days turned into weeks, and weeks into months, as the three found familiarity in their peaceful routine.

The jubilant moment arrived when Mahadeva, pleased with Grishna's fervent devotion, bestowed upon her a precious gift – a healthy son. Sudharma, overjoyed that his lineage would continue, celebrated the arrival of his heir.

However, the shadow of jealousy soon cast itself upon Sudheha's heart, just as her husband had predicted. Grishna's motherhood, while bringing happiness to the *ashram*, became a source of inner mayhem for Sudheha as envy took root within her.

As Sudheha cradled her stepson for the first time and gazed into the infant's eyes, a concoction of emotions flooded her heart. In that tender moment, as she held the baby close, Sudheha could not help but compare the scene to the one she had always envisioned for herself – a good fortune that had eluded her.

With each delicate movement of the child in her arms, Sudheha's thoughts rebounded in the soundless chambers of her mind, 'Why have I not been blessed with motherhood? It should have been my arms cradling my own son. Why is it that my sister has been granted the joy of bearing a son, and not me?' The infant, gurgling, blissfully unaware, became an unwitting symbol of Sudheha's unfulfilled maternal aspirations.

As the years passed, Grishna and Sudharma's son matured into a handsome young man, becoming the focal point of their lives. His presence in the *ashram* brought immense joy and further strengthened the bond between Grishna and Sudharma as they revelled in the shared experience of parenthood.

Despite Grishna's persistent efforts to bridge the emotional gap, time failed to alleviate Sudheha's intense jealousy. On the contrary, the passing years seemed only to exacerbate the envy festering within her heart. Though Grishna endeavoured to extend kindness and care to her elder sister, Sudheha remained obstinately unreceptive to the gestures of love from both Sudharma and Grishna.

The imminent marriage of Grishna and Sudharma's son marked a significant milestone, and while the *ashram* bustled with preparations for the wedding, Sudheha found herself increasingly isolated, her longing for motherhood intensifying with each passing moment. The sight of the young man, a living reminder of the familial joy she had been denied, became unbearable. Sudheha, unable to tolerate even a fleeting glimpse of the child, withdrew further into the shadows of her own sentiments, distancing herself from the celebrations.

Grishna compassionately instructed her new daughter-in-law to extend special care to Sudheha, in addition to her customary family duties. However, consumed by unchecked jealousy and rage, Sudheha succumbed to the dark impulses festering within her.

One fateful day, her malignant broodings reached a breaking point, leading her to commit a heinous act born of her uncontrolled antagonism. Sudheha took the life of her own sister's son, cruelly dismembering his body. With a disturbed mind and heart clouded by bitterness, Sudheha sought to conceal the grisly evidence of her crime. She disposed of the dismembered remains by submerging them into the very pond that held sacred significance for Grishna's worship rituals. The pond, which symbolized untainted piety for Grishna, now harboured the chilling secret of Sudheha's malevolence.

The daughter-in-law, horrified by the gruesome discovery of flesh and blood on their marital bed, rushed to Grishna with the devastating news. By the time Sudheha returned home, the room was engulfed in the deep hues of sorrow, the two women weeping copiously. Sudheha joined them, shedding a few crocodile tears, her emotions painted with a deceptive layer of false concern.

Upon returning home, Sudharma witnessed a heart-wrenching scene: the three women of his family engulfed in tears. The grave news struck him with insurmountable sorrow and he sought consolation in the wisdom that had guided him through life's trials. He addressed the three women, 'Dearest family, I know that our hearts are heavy with grief, and the pain we feel is immeasurable. However, we must remember the strength that lies in an unfaltering spiritual fidelity to Mahadeva. In times of despair, our faith becomes a beacon of hope, guiding us through these darkest hours.'

He urged them to channel their sorrow into their worship, emphasizing that the connection they shared with Mahadeva would serve as a balm for their wounded souls. Grishna, with a pain that cut deep into her soul, persevered in her allegiance to Mahadeva.

The pond by the *ashram*, a witness to the joyous moments of worship and celebration, became a poignant backdrop for Grishna's silent convalescence. She offered flowers, lit incense and chanted prayers for Mahadeva.

A span of days drifted by, each marked by the sombre rhythm of worship within the *ashram*. As Grishna treaded towards the pond, she scarcely believed her eyes. What awaited her was beyond this dimension of comprehension – a surreal scene that blurred the lines between reality and beyond.

There, by the rippling waters of the pond, stood her beloved son, alive and well.

The miraculous sight held her in suspended disbelief. Her heart raced, and tears welled in her eyes, as if unsure whether to surrender to joy or fear that this might all be an ephemeral dream.

Overwhelmed by the surge of emotions, Grishna hastened towards her son. As she embraced him, tears cascaded down her cheeks – tears of joy that mingled with a few of the intense sorrow she had been enveloped in. Her son too felt the warmth of his mother's love, a love that had transcended the boundaries of life and death.

'Mother, I have returned to you by the generous blessings of Mahadeva,' her son spoke, his voice evincing genuine gratitude. In that moment, Grishna held her son close, caressing the reality of his presence as if afraid the dream might shatter.

The family's prayers, Grishna's abiding zeal and the benevolence of Mahadeva had together orchestrated a reunion that defied the natural order. A torrent of questions overwhelmed her and she inquired, 'What had happened to you, son? Why did you leave me and go?'

The young man recounted the harrowing tale of his demise and the inexplicable return from the clutches of death.

Horror gripped Grishna's heart, contrasting sharply with the elation of having her son restored to her. In that moment, she realized the depths to which jealousy and malice could drive even the closest of kin.

Overwhelmed with gratitude and awe for the godly intervention that had brought her son back to life, Grishna prostrated herself before the *lingams* she had diligently crafted from sand. Her heart swelled with unbridled joy as she profusely thanked Mahadeva.

As Grishna fell to her knees in reverence, a warm glow enveloped their surroundings, signalling the arrival of Mahadeva in response to her earnest prayers. The epitome of benevolence stood before her, casting a mesmerizing glow. Mahadeva, with His serene countenance, surveyed the devoted mother and her son before Him.

With an empathetic smile, Mahadeva spoke to Grishna, 'Your enduring love towards me has brought your son back to you.' His words resonated through the depths of her soul. She fell at His feet.

'I am blessed, O Lord,' she said. 'No words can truly express all that I am feeling at this very moment. Not only has my son returned to me, but by Your blessings, I am also fortunate enough to lay my eyes on the Lord of Lords Himself. I can ask for nothing more in this life or any other life,' she uttered, her heart overflowing with humble and sincere dedication.

Mahadeva's mien darkened as He addressed Sudheha's unsettling actions: 'Your sister was the cause of all your pain. While your belief in me never faltered, your sister was not regular in her daily rituals and prayers. She was consumed by jealousy and the immense hatred that she was fostering towards you. She shall be punished for the sins she has committed,' He proclaimed.

As the impending judgement hung in the air, Grishna, driven by her kind heart and familial love, approached Mahadeva with a plea for mercy. 'O Lord, whose mercy and wisdom transcend mortal understanding, I humbly beseech You on behalf of my sister,' she implored Mahadeva. prostrating herself before Him. 'Despite the pain she has caused and the sins she has committed, I implore You to forgive her. In her heart, she is but human, and her actions were born of the struggles she faced. Please acquiesce to my request, Mahadeva, and let Your mercy wash away her transgressions.' In the face of Mahadeva's righteous anger, Grishna was determined to seek redemption for her sister.

After a brief pause, Mahadeva acknowledged Grishna's plea and the depths of her love for her sister, saying, 'Grishna, your love and compassion attest to the strength of familial bonds. Your sister shall be granted forgiveness, for your heart speaks of a love that transcends even the gravest of errors. As a mother and sister, your compassion and nurturing comportment has moved me, and I shall absolve Sudheha of her sins. May this act of forgiveness be a testament to the transformative power of love.'

With Mahadeva's pronouncement, Grishna felt an enormous sense of relief surge through her. The interposition had not only saved her sister from the consequences of her actions but had also reaffirmed the boundless nature of mercy.

Sudheha, overwhelmed by the unexpected mercy bestowed upon her, fell first at the feet of the benevolent deity and then at Grishna's feet. Tears streamed down her eyes, carrying with them the burden of remorse and gratitude. In that sacred moment, forgiveness became the salve for wounds inflicted, and the mercy of Mahadeva embraced even the repentant heart of Sudheha.

In the remaining chapters of her mortal journey, Sudheha, now with a heart absolved through ceaseless prayer, embarked on a path of redemption and love. Much to the joy of Sudharma and Grishna, the formerly tormented soul found solace in extending her affections to Grishna's son as if he were her own, and to his wife as the daughter they never had, eagerly making up for all the time lost. Her genuine efforts were dedicated to strengthening the kinship that had earlier been strained by the shadows of her own transgressions.

Her heart now overflowed with gratitude. Sudheha found herself thanking Mahadeva for opening her eyes, purging her soul of devious intentions, and granting her the chance to rebuild and cherish the familial ties she had nearly destroyed.

In a heartfelt plea, Grishna implored Mahadeva to grace the very spot where her son had been miraculously resurrected, a testament to the Lord's boundless kindness and enduring love for His devoted followers, ' O Mahadeva, on this sacred ground where my son was granted a second chance at life, I beseech You to grace us with Your continued presence. Let this place be forever sanctified by the memory of Your kindness and the unending love You have for all your children, both the devoted and those who have momentarily strayed from their path.'

Mahadeva obliged.

*In other versions of this story, Grishna is known as Dhushma* or Ghushma. In one version she is referred to as Kusuma and is Sudharma's first wife. The narrative depicts Kusuma as the loyal spouse who experiences the devastating loss of her son. However, it is the jealous second wife of Sudharma who commits the tragic act of murdering her son.

*In alternative versions of this legend, the narrative takes a* different turn as Mahadeva, revealing the truth about the demise of Grishna's son, prepares to wield His *trishul* to punish Sudheha. However, Grishna intervenes, falling at the Lord's feet and fervently praying for her sister's absolution. Touched by Grishna's fierce love for her sister, despite the betrayal, Mahadeva grants her a boon. In response, Grishna requests Him to establish His presence on the banks of the pond where she was reunited with her resurrected son.

Belief holds that Sudharma and his wives resided at the foothills of the Devagiri Hills, a correlation pointing to Daulatabad, formerly recognized as Devagiri. Significantly, this city is close to the temple.

This temple is also known as Dhushmeshwar and is situated near the Ellora Caves in Aurangabad, Maharashtra.

It is the twelfth *jyotirlinga*.

*Jyotirmaya-dwadasha-linga-kanam*
*Shivatmanam prokta-midam kramena*
*Stotram pathitva manujo-ati-bhaktya*
*Phalam tadalokya nijam bhajechha*

This prayer, which elaborates on
The twelve resplendent *jyotirlingas*,
If recited with devotion,
Would bear the desired fruit.
– from the *Dwadasa Jyotirlinga Stotram*, Adi Shankaracharya

# Fascinating Facts, Practices and Beliefs about the *Jyotirlinga*s

## SOMNATH

- According to the *Skanda Purana*, the inception of the original Somnath Temple dates back to approximately 79,925,105 years.
- Further, the text states that the Somnath Temple undergoes a change in nomenclature with each cycle of world reconstruction or *yuga*. It was initially built in gold by Somaraj during the *satya yuga*, followed by Ravana, who built it in silver during the *treta yuga*. Lord Krishna chose sandalwood for its construction in the *dwapara yuga*, and in the *Kali yuga*, King Bhimadeva built the temple with stone.

This sequence reveals a fascinating correlation between each *yuga* and the chosen construction material for the temple.

- Referenced in the *Rig Veda*, the term Somnath translates to 'The Protector of the Moon God.' Despite enduring many instances of destruction, the Somnath Temple is renowned as the 'Shrine Eternal'.
- It is believed that the Somnath Temple secretly houses within its ancient structure, the *syamantaka mani* or the 'Philosopher's Stone'. Legend suggests that this stone possesses alchemical properties, purportedly capable of transmuting base metals into gold. Furthermore, it is believed to emit radiation, generating a magnetic field that enables it to hover above the ground. Lord Krishna was once wrongly accused of having stolen this gem.
- The Somnath Temple site is revered as the convergence of three sacred rivers: Kapila, Hiran and the mythical Saraswati, as they meet the Arabian Sea on India's western coast. This junction, known as Triveni Sangam, is where Somaraj is said to have bathed after worshipping Lord Shiva to restore his waning radiance.
- The confluence at Triveni Ghat symbolizes the journey of human life, from birth to death, and holds deep significance in Hindu mythology and scriptures like the Ramayana and Mahabharata. Triveni Sangam is believed to possess purifying powers, with a bath at this hallowed junction thought to facilitate *moksha*, the liberation of the soul.
- Prabhas Patan, the site of the Somnath Temple, is considered to be the place where the members of the Yadava clan (Lord Krishna's kinsmen) fought among themselves, thus causing

the annihilation of their own lineage. Near the Sangam area lies the sacred site of Lord Krishna's departure from his mortal form, known as Dehotsarg (meaning 'leaving the body') or Golokdham Teerth. Located along the banks of the River Hiran, this *teerth* is home to two main temples – the Geeta Temple and the Lakshmi Narayan Temple. It is believed that the Geeta Temple marks the exact spot where Lord Krishna attained his final rest.

- Char Dham Yatra, first undertaken by the revered Adi Shankaracharya, is a famous pilgrimage route established by him: Ramanathaswamy Temple in Tamil Nadu, Puri Jagannath in Odisha, Somnath in Gujarat and Badrinath in Uttarakhand. Every Hindu pilgrim must travel this circuit at least once in their lifetime in order to attain *moksha*.
- The Somnath Temple is constructed in the Chalukya style of architecture.
- The temple is located on a site where there is a continuous stretch of water directly from the Somnath seashore to Antarctica, without any intervening land. An inscription stating the same can be found on one of the pillars in the temple. This pillar is known as *banastambha* or the 'Arrow Pillar'. It is one of the pillars installed to protect the Somnath Temple from the sea. Written in Sanskrit, the inscription states that the temple stands at such a point on the Indian landmass that it is the first point on land in the north from the South Pole at a particular longitude.
- The Somnath Temple has endured multiple instances of looting and plundering throughout history, including invasions by Mahmud of Ghazni in 1026, Allauddin Khilji in

1297, Mohammed Begeda in 1479, Muzaffar Shah II in 1503 and Aurangazeb in 1701. Despite these challenges, the temple has been reconstructed each time, standing today as a resilient monument for believers to visit and worship the deity.

- To address the damage inflicted by historical events, Rani Ahalyabai Holkar, a devout follower of Shiva, embarked on the reconstruction of the Somnath Temple in 1783. Following India's independence from British rule, Sardar Vallabhbhai Patel, along with renowned temple architect Prabhashankar Oghadbhai of Palitana, led further renovations, shaping the Somnath Temple into its present form.
- The Somnath *jyotirlinga* was reinstated on 11 May 1951, by India's then-president, Dr Rajendra Prasad, and remains intact to this day.

## MALLIKARJUNA

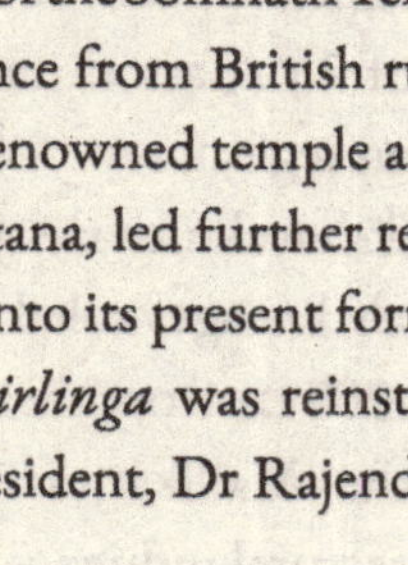

- The Mallikarjuna Temple is also one of the fifty-one *shaktipeetha*s present in India. This temple is unique as it is one of the only three sites in India where a *jyotirlinga* and *shaktipeetha* are housed in the same temple complex.

The other two are the Baidyanath Temple in Deogarh, Jharkhand, and the Kashi Vishwanath Temple in Varanasi, Uttar Pradesh.

- This temple's origin can be traced back to some of the first rulers of south India. The corresponding proof can be found in the inscriptions on the walls of the structure. One of the earliest known inscriptions can be found in Pulumavi's Nashik inscription of 2 CE, associated with the Satavahana dynasty of the Deccan region.
- Some say that the Ikshavaku dynasty ('descendants of the moon'); Lord Rama's lineage, ruled close to the Srisailam Temple during 200–300 CE from their capital of Vijayapuri, and that is how the Mallikarjuna Temple received its patronage and architectural influence.
- Other dynasties that provided patronage to this temple include the Pallavas (248–575 CE), the Kakatiyas (953–1323 CE), the Kadambas (340–450 CE), the Chalukyas (624–848 CE) and the Reddi kings (1325–1448 CE), whose reigns comprised 'the golden age' of Srisailam.
- Most of the major renovations that the Mallikarjuna Temple has undergone are said to have been carried out under the orders of the Vijayanagara rulers between 1336 and 1678 CE.
- The construction of the *gopuram* of this temple is attributed to different historical figures according to varying accounts. Some sources claim that Chhatrapati Shivaji Maharaj built it in 1674 CE, while others suggest that it was erected during the reign of Krishnadevaraya. Chhatrapati Shivaji may have commissioned additional renovations rather than ordered the construction of the *gopuram*.

- The Mallikarjuna Temple has found repeated mentions in various ancient texts, each adding to its sacred lore. The *Agni Purana* recounts the tale of the *asura*-king Hiranyakashipu, who engaged in penance at this very site, seeking the blessings of Lord Shiva. The *Skanda Purana* narrates the visit of Lord Rama and Sita to this temple during their period of *vanavas*. Similarly, the Mahabharata chronicles the sojourn of the Pandavas and their wife, Draupadi, at this revered site, seeking solace during their exile following the infamous game of dice with their cousins, the Kauravas.
- Sri Adi Shankaracharya is said to have composed his famous poem '*Shivananda Lahiri*' at this temple.

## MAHAKALESHWAR

- Ujjain, situated on the banks of the River Kshipra, holds the distinction of being one of the venues for the renowned Kumbha Mela, an event that occurs once every twelve years. During the famous episode of *samudra manthan* or the churning of the Ocean of Milk, which both the *deva*s and the *asura*s took part in, Lord Vishnu took the form of the enticing maiden, Mohini, to trick the *asuras* and give the *amrit* or the nectar of immortality only to the *devas*. A fight ensued between the two factions and, during this scuffle, four drops of the divine nectar fell from the *kumbh* and landed at Prayagraj, Haridwar, Ujjain and Nashik.

Some say that the *asuras* and *devas* fought each other for the possession of the *amrit* for twelve days and twelve nights and it was during this period that the four drops of nectar fell on earth. As twelve days of the *devas* are equivalent to as many years on earth, the Kumbha Mela takes place once every twelve years. Thousands of people visit the sites of the Kumbh Mela to bathe and wash their sins away and worship the *devas* – on the banks of the River Godavari in Nashik, River Kshipra in Ujjain, River Ganga in Haridwar and the Triveni Sangam in Prayagraj.

- As per the *Bhagavata Purana*, Rishi Sandipani established his *gurukul* at this very spot, and young princes from far and wide enrolled here to learn the ancient texts, the art of war and all the other skills required for them to rule their kingdoms efficiently. Lord Krishna and his elder brother, Balarama, are said to have attended this *gurukul* to complete their education.
- It is one of the nineteen *maha shaktipeethas*.
- Built in the eighteenth century, the Mahakaleshwar Temple is a breathtaking blend of Bhumika, Chalukya and Maratha styles of architecture.
- The phallic structure at this temple is referred to as 'Dakshinamurti', meaning that this *jyotirlinga* faces south. All the others face east.

- The Mahakaleshwar temple is renowned for its '*bhasma aarti*' that is performed every day at 4 a.m. The speciality of this *aarti* is that it is performed entirely with ash (*bhasma*), which denotes the transient nature of life.
- Coins from the kingdom of Ujjain, which can be traced back to 4–3 BCE, have the figure of Lord Shiva imprinted on them.
- The temple, having been destroyed a few times by marauders, was finally restored by the Marathas when their rule was established in the eighteenth century. The renovation we witness today can be credited to Ranoji Shinde.
- The Mahakaleshwar Temple features several times in various ancient texts, including the *Purana*s, but its most detailed descriptions lie in the many works of Kalidasa.

## OMKARESHWAR

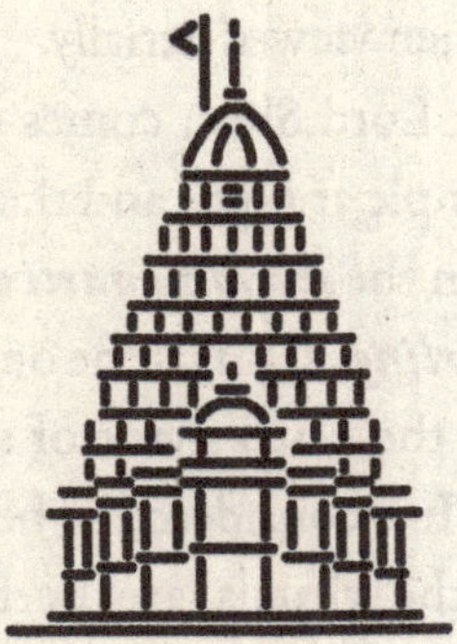

- The temple is situated on an island on the River Narmada, known as Mandhata or Shivapuri, which is unique in resembling the sacred symbol 'Om' (ॐ) in its shape. This symbol, revered as the most sacred sound in Shaivism, symbolizes Lord Shiva and is also emblematic of the holy Trinity, i.e., Brahma, Vishnu and Shiva. This *jyotirlinga* is situated at the confluence of the rivers Narmada and Kaveri. Perched on a cliff overlooking the rushing rapids of the River Narmada, this ancient temple holds a sacred presence. According to beliefs, the River Narmada is considered to be the daughter of Lord Shiva.

- The temple, constructed in the Nagara architectural style, is a notable example of late medieval architecture, prevalent from the thirteenth to sixteenth centuries, especially during the Peshwa period. Its origins trace back to the ninth to thirteenth centuries, attributed to the Parmara rulers of Malwa. However, the structure we see today is believed to have been erected by the Holkars in the eleventh century.
- Omkareshwar is situated between two lofty hills that form the 'Om' shape when viewed aerially.
- Many believe that Lord Shiva comes down to sleep at the Omkareshwar Temple at night and that is why the priests at the temple perform the *shayana aarti* every night.
- Of the twelve *jyotirlinga*s, this is the only structure that does not seem to be in the usual shape of a phallic structure, as most *lingam*s are. It is considered to be shapeless.
- In this temple, the rituals are performed by different groups of priests. The morning *puja* is conducted by the temple trust, the daytime *puja*s are performed by the

Scindia family and, finally, the evening *puja* is performed by the Holkars.

- There is a path that traces the entire circumference of the holy island, spanning 16 km. It is called the Omkareshwara *parikrama*. Walking the path that encircles the entire island is considered highly auspicious and is believed to bring great blessings. The path passes by numerous temples, *ashrams* and villages, bringing pilgrims additional blessings along the way.
- The Amreshwar *lingam* is said to lie exactly midway between the source of the River Narmada and its final destination as it drains into the Arabian Sea. Hence, this spot is often considered to be the *nabhi sthal* or the navel of the river.
- It is believed that when King Mandhata of the Ikshvaku dynasty and an ancestor of Lord Rama, built and worshipped the *jyotirlinga* at this spot, the holy island used to glow lustrously. When Sage Narada asked Lord Shiva about this, Lord Shiva is said to have told him that the island changes its appearance in every *yuga*. First, in the *satya yuga*, it sparkled like a precious gem; in the *treta yuga*, it was a mountain of gold; in the *dwapara yuga*, the island was composed of copper and, finally, in the *Kali yuga*, the island is made of rock.
- Adi Shankaracharya's guru, Govinda Bhagavatpada, is believed to have lived in a cave near the temple.

## KEDARESHWAR

- Due to its location in the lower Shivalik ranges of the Himalayas in Uttarakhand, the Kedarnath Temple closes during the harsh winter months due to heavy snowfall. During this time, the Shiva idol is transported to Ukhimath for worship. It is re-installed at the Kedarnath Temple during the month of Vaishakh according to the Hindu calendar, when the temple reopens for worship.
- Another circuit of temples, also referred to as *Char Dham Yatra* or *Chhota Char Dham Yatra*, is in Uttarakhand. This *yatra* entails visiting and worshipping at the Gangotri, Yamunotri, Badrinath and Kedarnath temples. This pilgrimage route is said to be over 1,200 years old. The shrine at Yamunotri commemorates the origin of the sacred River Yamuna. Gangotri denotes the place where Ganga descended to earth from the heavens to wash away the sins of King Bhagiratha's ancestors. It is believed that one must travel the *Char Dham Yatra* at least once in one's lifetime.
- Originally believed to have been constructed by the Pandavas during the events of the Mahabharata, the

Kedarnath Temple underwent a rebuilding process led by Adi Shankaracharya. He spent numerous years near the temple and eventually embarked on his final journey into the higher Himalayan ranges to attain salvation.

- King Kedar, known to have been just and kind, is said to have ruled the region during the *satya yuga*. The temple is thought to have been named after him in recognition of his virtues.
- Scientists have claimed that the Kedarnath Temple was submerged in snow, in what they call a mini ice age, for about 400 years or so, during 1300–1900 CE. Yet, the temple structure still stands tall and unaffected.
- The Bhairavnath Temple, popularly referred to as the Bhairon Baba Mandir, is situated in the vicinity of the Kedarnath Temple. Bhairon Baba is considered to be the guardian deity of the Kedarnath *jyotirlinga*. This protective deity is also referred to as *kshetrapal*.
- The Kedarnath Temple is part of a revered temple circuit known as the '*Panch Kedar*'. This circuit comprises five Shiva temples located in the Garhwal region of the Himalayas, along the banks of the River Mandakini, in Uttarakhand. Pilgrims must adhere to a specific order when visiting these temples. The journey begins with the Kedarnath Temple, followed by the Tunganath Temple, Madhyamaheshwar Temple, Rudranath Temple, and finally the Kalpeshwar Temple. This sequence is to be strictly followed.
- The priesthood responsible for conducting ceremonies at the Kedarnath Temple exclusively comprises members of

the Veerashaiva community from Karnataka. The leader of this priesthood, known as the 'Rawal', does not personally conduct any rituals but instead delegates all ceremonial duties to subordinates, adhering to a long-standing tradition of the temple. Rituals at the temple are conducted solely in Kannada, a linguistic and procedural tradition that has remained unchanged over the centuries. During the winter closure of the Kedarnath Temple, the Rawal accompanies the phallic structure to Ukhimath.

- The Kedarnath Temple is the highest of the *jyotirlinga*s, at an altitude of approximately 3,582 m above sea level.
- This temple stands as a testament to both architectural ingenuity and divine protection. Crafted from massive stone slabs, the temple rests upon a sturdy rectangular platform, elevating it approximately 6 feet above the ground. What truly distinguishes its construction is the interlocking technique employed, seamlessly joining the stones without the need for adhesives. These colossal slabs, measuring around 12 feet in thickness, fortify the temple against the elements of nature, ensuring its endurance even in the face of adverse weather conditions.
- This architectural marvel has endured the test of time, surviving over a millennium without succumbing to decay or deterioration. Remarkably, it has weathered a mini ice age and, more recently, the devastating floods of 2013, which swept away the surrounding settlements and shops. Despite the havoc wreaked by nature, the temple remained unscathed, a testament to the protective embrace of Mahadeva.

## BHIMASHANKAR

- The Bhimashankar Temple was built in the Nagara style of architecture with a touch of influence from the Indo-Aryan style and dates back to the eighteenth century.
- The phallic structure installed in this temple is quite thick and hence, it has earned the name of 'Moteshwar Mahadeva'.
- The dome of this temple is believed to have been built by Nana Phadnavis in the eighteenth century.
- The Bhimashankar Temple is thought to be the source of the River Bhima, also referred to as River Bhimarathi, that flows south-east and merges with the River Krishna.
- While the structure of this temple was built in the eighteenth century, the walls of the temple complex have been inscribed with ancient inscriptions dating back to the thirteenth century.
- The shrine of Kamalaja is situated very close to the Bhimashankar Temple. It is the shrine of Goddess Parvati, who is believed to have aided Mahadeva in the battle against Tripurasura.
- Folklore suggests that Bhima, the second Pandava prince, married Hidimbi, an *asura* princess at this temple.

## VISHWESHWAR

- Tradition holds that those who draw their last breath in the sacred city of Kashi ascend directly to the gates of heaven. This belief has persisted since ancient times, as evidenced in our epics and *Purana*s. It is customary for individuals, including royalty relinquishing their thrones, to enter the final stages of their lives – *vanaprastha* and *sanyasa* – to embark on a pilgrimage to Kashi. In Hindu theology, it is firmly believed that departing from this holy city leads to *moksha* (salvation). Those who pass away in Kashi are liberated from the cycle of birth, death and rebirth, thus merging with the Supreme Being or '*Paramatman*'. Over time, many homes have been established in Kashi, allowing people to spend their final days in anticipation of breathing their last in this sacred land of Mahadeva. The phrase '*kashyam maranam mukti*' emphasizes that dying in Kashi equals attaining salvation. It is believed that in Kashi individuals attain salvation as Mahadeva whispers the *Taraka Mantra* to them as they take their final breath. This liberation extends to individuals of all origins.

- Another belief and practice related to the pilgrimage to Kashi involves visiting Rameswaram. It is believed that a pilgrimage to Kashi will not yield its full benefits unless one also visits Rameswaram. According to this tradition, to complete the Kashi Yatra successfully, pilgrims must first visit Rameswaram and collect sand from its shores. Upon reaching Kashi, they are required to deposit this sand into the sacred Ganga and collect water from it. Afterwards, they must return to Rameswaram and perform an *abhishekam*, or ritual bathing, where *gangajal* (water from the Ganga) is poured over the Rameswaram *jyotirlinga*. Only after completing this ritual, it is said, will one's Kashi Yatra be considered complete and fruitful, earning the designation of a *sampoorna yatra*.
- Another myth surrounding this holy city entails that Kashi sits on the tip of Lord Shiva's *trishul*, implying that the 'land of Shiva' is not on earth but is in fact hovering above it! It is further believed that there are three temples that sit on the three tips of the *trishul*: Omkareshwar in the north, Vishweshwar in the middle and Kedareshwar in the south.
- As per traditional folklore, there are eight Kaal Bhairavas, who are known to be the guardians of the city. They are also known as the Ashta Dikkugalu. The temples for these deities are present in the eight cardinal directions, scattered across the city. Kaal Bhairava is said to sport a tiger-skin cloth, hold a sword in his right hand and the head of an *asura* in his left hand. His *vahana* is a dog.
- Another common myth suggests that one will never see an eagle fly over this city or hear a lizard clicking. The story

behind this belief is linked to that of the Rameswaram *jyotirlinga*. After Lord Rama had vanquished Ravana and wished to atone for his sin of *brahmin-hatya* in Rameswaram, he sent his trusted companion, Hanuman, to bring a *lingam* that he could install in Rameswaram. When Hanuman arrived in Kashi, he was aided by a *garuda* (eagle) and a lizard in identifying the *lingam*. However, Hanuman inadvertently took the *lingam* without seeking permission from Kaal Bhairava, the guardian deity of Kashi. This action sparked a fierce battle between the two, which was interrupted by the *deva*s. In a fit of rage, Kaal Bhairava cursed the *garuda*, prohibiting it from ever flying over Kashi again, and the lizard, condemning it to perpetual silence within the city.

- It is also believed that Lord Shiva and His consort, Goddess Parvati, visit Kashi to bathe at its holy ghats. Similarly, Lord Vishnu and Goddess Lakshmi are said to frequent the ghats too. Some legends suggest that even Lord Brahma visits Kashi at noon for the same purpose. This belief underscores the significance of the *madhyanika snanam*, or the 'bath at noon', in the Ganga, which is considered highly auspicious. Consequently, every pilgrim endeavours to immerse themselves in the waters of the sacred river at least once in their lifetime.
- Varanasi is also referred to as the 'City of Ghats'. A 'ghat' is the term used to refer to a flight of steps leading down to the river. In Varaṇasi, there are about 100 ghats, each of which has a special story. Out of these, some of the most popular ones are:

- *Assi Ghat*: The first ghat where people often bathe before performing their prayers to Mahadeva. It is located at the southernmost tip of Varanasi's riverfront, at the confluence point of the rivers Ganga and Assi.
- *Manikarnika Ghat*: Dubbed as 'the burning ghat', this is where bodies are cremated round the clock, twenty-four hours a day! Most cremations are done here, the rest being performed at the Harishchandra Ghat.
- *Harishchandra Ghat*: Another ghat well known for cremations of bodies. It is at these two ghats that one can grasp the profound meaning of life, witnessing it come full circle.
- *Dashashwamedha Ghat*: This ghat is located at one of the entrances of the Kashi Vishwanath temple. It is renowned for hosting the daily Ganga *aarti*, a mesmerizing spectacle that every visitor to Kashi must witness. According to belief, this auspicious ghat was created by Lord Brahma to welcome Lord Shiva. Legend has it that during a *yagna* conducted at this ghat, Lord Brahma sacrificed numerous horses, hence its befitting name.
- *Chet Singh Ghat*: It houses the Chet Singh Qila, the fort from where Maharaja Chet Singh, the ruler of Varanasi, waged war against the first British Governor of the Presidency of Fort William (Bengal), Warren Hastings. Although he was vanquished by the British forces, Maharaja Chet Singh was said to have escaped unscathed from the battle.
- *Hanuman Ghat*: This ghat is believed to have been built by Lord Rama for his most loving disciple, Hanuman.
- *Scindia Ghat*: Built in 1835, the ghat includes a partially flooded shrine of Lord Shiva. The Ratneshwar Shiva

Temple, also known as the 'leaning Shiva temple', finds itself partially submerged in the Ganges due to its inability to withstand the weight of the ghat and its 150-year-old construction. The ghat itself is named after Maharani Baijabaai Scindia, a former queen of Gwalior. It is considered to be the birthplace of Agni.

- *Tulsi Ghat*: Named after the saint-poet Tulsi Das, this ghat houses the place where he stayed while composing his famous *Ramcharitamanas* and *Hanuman Chalisa*.
- *Mahanirvani Ghat*: It is a long-standing belief that the Buddha once bathed at this ghat. Other believe that the famed Sage Kapila lived here for a time.
- *Raj Ghat*: This ghat lies at the other end from Assi Ghat. Situated at the confluence point of the Ganga and Varuna rivers, this ghat is considered to have immense religious importance. Lord Vishnu is said to reside at this home of the Adi Keshava Vishnu Temple.

- As per the *Kashi Khand*, the Kashi Vishwanath temple was formerly known as the Moksh Lakshmi Vilas Temple with five *mandaps*.
- According to the same scripture, as Lord Shiva extolled the temple's greatness to Indra, the *saptarishi*s surrounded them. This belief translates into a nightly ritual where seven priests gather to perform *aarti* in Lord Shiva's honour daily at 7 p.m., an unmissable spectacle for temple visitors. Known as the *saptarishi aarti*, this tradition is at least 750 years old.
- Unlike most temples in India where devotees are restricted from entering the sanctum sanctorum, the Kashi Vishwanath

Temple is an exception, allowing worshippers access to this sacred space.

- This temple, traced back to the eleventh century, is said to have been repeatedly plundered by invaders, and rebuilt.
- The Kashi Vishwanath Temple, in its sanctum sanctorum, has three *gopuram*s covered in pure gold. The precious metal for the dome was contributed by Maharaja Ranjit Singh of Punjab.
- There are various temples in the holy city of Kashi that are worshipped as *jyotirlinga*s. Tradition dictates that worshipping the phallic structures at these temples is equivalent to worshipping each of the *jyotiringa*s themselves. This indicates the divinity of the ancient temple city of Kashi. The *jyotirlinga*s are worshipped in Kashi within the following temples:
    - Somnath at the Someshwar Temple, Manmandir Ghat.
    - Mallikarjuna at the Tripurantakeshwar Temple, Sigra.
    - Mahakaleshwar at the Mahakaleshwar Temple, Daranagar.
    - Omkareshwar at the Omkareshwar Temple, Machhodari.
    - Baidyanath at the Bajinatheshwar Temple, Kamachha.
    - Bhimashankar at the Bhimeshwar Kashi Karvat Temple, Govindpura.
    - Rameshwar at the Ganeshwar Temple, Man Mandir Ghat.
    - Nageshwar at the Nageshwar Temple, Bhonsle Ghat.
    - Trayambakeshwar at the Trayambakeshwar Temple, Godowlia.
    - Kedareshwar at the Kedareshwar Temple, Kedar Ghat.
    - Grishneshwar at the Grishneshwar Mahadev temple in the premises of the Kamakhya Devi Temple, Kamachha.

## TRAYAMBAKESHWAR

- The Trayambakeshwar or Trimbakeshwar Temple was originally built by Peshwa Nanasaheb, also known as Peshwa Balaji Baji Rao, between 1755 and 1786 CE. Legend has it that Nanasaheb, believing that the Trayambakeshwar *jyotirlinga* was not hollow, lost a bet and, in response, built this architecturally significant temple.
- The temple used to house a lustrous diamond, known as the 'eye of the idol'. Considered to be one of the twenty greatest diamonds of the world, the Nassak Diamond is a 43.38-carat (the original uncut stone was approximately 89 carats) precious stone that once adorned the golden crown of the idol. Deriving its name from 'Nashik', the diamond has a long and interesting history, beginning from the seizing of the mines of Golconda by the Mughals in 1687 CE to the Third Anglo-Maratha War in 1818 CE, resulting in Bajirao II surrendering the diamond as the spoils of war to the British. Today, the radiant diamond is among the distinguished pieces in the collection of Lebanese millionaire and gem collector Robert Mouawad.

- The bejewelled golden crown that the Nassak Diamond used to be a part of can still be viewed in the temple every Monday from 4–5 p.m., when it is ceremoniously placed on the phallic structure. The crown is adorned with diamonds, pearls, emeralds and other precious stones, which are believed to have been owned and worn by the Pandavas.
- The birthplace of Lord Hanuman in the Anjaneri mountains is only 7 km from the Trayambakeshwar Temple.
- Also referred to as the 'black stone temple', it is constructed entirely from basalt, a type of volcanic lava rock. The architectural style of the temple blends elements of Indo-Aryan and Hemadpanti styles. The Hemadpanti style, named after the prime minister Hemadpant (1259–74 CE) of the court of the Seuna Yadavas of Devagiri, is characterized by intricate carvings depicting gods, goddesses, *yaksha*s and *apsara*s, and floral designs adorning the temple structure and pillars.
- The River Godavari originates at this place, in the foothills amid the three hills of Brahmagiri, Nilgiri and Kalagiri.
- The temple complex is home to numerous *teertham*s (wells). The Kushavarta Teertham is a well containing water from the River Godavari, said to have been secured by Rishi Gautama. The Varaha Teertham is another well, purportedly used by Lord Vishnu prior to taking the form of the *varaha*.
- It is the venue of the Simhasta Kumbha Mela, which is held once every twelve years.

- The uniqueness of the Trayambakeshwar *jyotirlinga* lies in its phallic structure, distinguished by three faces representing the holy Trinity: Lord Brahma, the Creator; Lord Vishnu, the Preserver; and, of course, Lord Shiva, the Destroyer.

## BAIDYANATH

- The Baidyanath Temple is also one of the fifty-one *shaktipeetha*s present in India. This temple is unique as it is one of the only three places in India where a *jyotirlinga* and *shaktipeetha* are housed in the same temple complex. The other such temples are the Mallikarjuna Temple of Srisailam in Kurnool, Andhra Pradesh, and the Kashi Vishwanath Temple in Varanasi.
- The name of the actual person who built this temple cannot be traced, but some believe that the temple was built by Puran Mal, an ancestor of the maharaja of Gidhaur, in 1596 CE.

## NAGESHWAR

- The *jyotirlinga* appears in the shape of a *trimukhi rudraksha* (three-faced sacred bead), facing south, while the temple faces east. The original temple complex is thought to be huge, but is believed to be submerged in the ocean.
- The current temple structure was designed by architect Subhash Bhoite, adhering to the principles of *vastu shastra*. Renovation work was overseen by Gulshan Kumar, founder of the T-Series music label, and his son Bhushan Kumar, the current chairman and managing director of T-Series.
- The temple is built in a manner that denotes the sleeping or lying down, i.e., '*shayanam*' pose of the human body. The *mahadwar* (main door) corresponds to the feet, the entrance porch to the arms, the *sabha mandapa* (prayer hall) to the abdomen, the *antarala* (sitting place of Nandi) to the chest, and the *garbhagriha* (sanctum sanctorum), where the Nageshwar *jyotirlinga* is installed, the head of the body.
- The Darukavanam mentioned in the origin story of the *jyotirlinga* was where the Pandavas are believed to have lived out some of their years of exile.

# RAMESHWAR

- The Ramanathaswamy Temple in Rameswaram, constructed in the twelfth century CE, exhibits the Dravidian style of architecture. Initially built by the Sethupathy and the Pandya dynasties, it underwent renovations by King Jeyaveera Cinkaiariyan of the Jaffna kingdom and his successor, Gunaveera Cinkaiariyan.
- The Chokkatan Mandapam, situated within the temple complex, holds the distinction of being the largest temple corridor globally. Comprising 1,212 pillars, each towering 30 feet high, it features intricate stone carvings depicting scenes from the *Purana*s and traditional designs. Remarkably, when viewed from one end, the convergence of all pillars creates a captivating optical illusion, a testament to the mastery of Tamil architects and builders.
- According to the *Skanda Purana*, there are sixty-four *teerthams* in and around the temple complex. While each has its own significance, twenty-four of these have been identified as the most important, and bathing in these is considered a form of penance to absolve oneself of sins.

Of these twenty-four *teerthams*, two are situated outside the temple complex and the remaining twenty-two are within the complex. It is believed that those who bathe in each of these twenty-two wells will be absolved of all their sins.

- Some believe that these twenty-two *teerthams* represent the twenty-two arrows in Lord Rama's quiver. They are:
  - *Agni Teertham*: Located near the beach, east of the Ramanathaswamy Temple.
  - *Setu Teertham*: Situated at Dhanushkodi, around 22 km from Rameswaram. The *Skanda Purana* proclaims that merely sleeping on the seashore at Rameswaram and bathing in the waters rids a person of all their sins and gains them entry into *vaikuntha loka*.
  - *Mahalakshmi Teertham*: Present inside the temple complex, it is believed to be the well in which King Yudhishthira bathed and performed penance to become a worthy ruler.
  - *Savitri Teertham*: It is believed to be the well where Sage Kashyapa got rid of his curse by taking a dip.
  - *Gayatri Teertham*: The well where Sage Kashyapa was absolved of his curse by taking a holy dip.
  - *Saraswati Teertham*: Sage Kashyapa had to bathe in this well too, to rid himself of his curse.
  - *Sethu Madhava Teertham*: If a person bathes in it, they will be blessed by Mahalakshmi Devi and be rid of impure thoughts.
  - *Gandhamadana Teertham*: According to the *Sthala Purana*, a person who bathes here will be rid of poverty.

- *Kavacha Teertham*: This well allows the person who bathes in it to be absolved of their sins.
- *Gavaya Teertham*: The person who bathes in it receives shelter under the mythical and majestic *kalpavriksha* tree in *swarga loka*.
- *Nala Teertham*: The person who bathes in it is blessed by Surya, the Sun God.
- *Neeka Teertham*: Taking a dip in this well is considered to be equivalent to having performed several *yagna*s and mastering *agni* yoga.
- *Shanku Teertham:* The well where Sage Vatsanabha bathed to absolve his sin of ingratitude.
- *Chakkara Teertham*: The well where Surya, the Sun God, bathed to turn his hands to gold so he could be lustrous and shine brighter.
- *Brahmahathi Vimochana Teertham*: The well that one is expected to bathe in to absolve oneself of the sin of *brahmin-hatya*.
- *Surya Teertham:* The well one is expected to bathe in to obtain the knowledge of one's past, present and future.
- *Chandra Teertham:* The well that also allows one to obtain knowledge of one's past, present and future.
- *Ganga Teertham:* It is the well where Raja Gananasuruthi bathed to attain the wisdom that he sought.
- *Yamuna Teertham*: Also where Raja Gananasuruthi bathed to attain the wisdom that he sought.
- *Gaya Teertham*: Once again, a well in which Raja Gananasuruthi bathed to attain the wisdom that he sought.

- *Shiva Teertham*: It entails absolution from the sin of *brahmin-hatya* and repenting of any ill-will spoken towards Lord Shiva.
- *Sadyamirtha Teertham*: The well in which one is to bathe to rid oneself of a curse.
- *Sarva Teertham*: The well in which Sutharishna bathed, to garner prosperity and rid himself of his congenital blindness.
- *Kodi Teertham*: According to the *Skanda Purana*, it is the well in which Lord Krishna bathed, to absolve himself of the sin of killing his uncle, Kansa.

## GRISHNESHWAR

- Featuring a south Indian architectural style and built of red stones, the Grishneshwar *jyotirlinga* temple is the smallest of the twelve *jyotirlinga* temples.
- Originally erected by Maloji Bhosle, the grandfather of Chhatrapati Shivaji Maharaj, this temple underwent reconstruction by Maharani Ahilyabai Holkar following its destruction during the Mughal era.

# 108 NAMES OF SHIVA

Shiva is known to have 1,008 names of which 108 are the most venerable. They are:

1. **Adiguru:** Supreme guru
2. **Adinatha:** Supreme lord
3. **Adiyogi:** Supreme yogi
4. **Aja:** Eternal/unborn
5. **Akshayaguna:** Of limitless attributes/qualities
6. **Anagha:** Faultless/pure
7. **Anantadrishti:** Of infinite vision
8. **Ashutosh:** Being who is easily gratified/fulfils wishes
9. **Augadh:** One who revels all the time
10. **Avyayaprabhu:** Imperishable
11. **Bhairava:** Destroyer of fear
12. **Bhalanetra:** One who has an eye in the forehead
13. **Bholenatha:** Lord of innocence/the innocent one
14. **Bhooteshwara:** One who has mastery over the elements
15. **Bhudeva:** Lord of earth
16. **Bhutapala:** Protector of supernatural beings
17. **Chandrapala:** Master of the moon

18. **Chandraprakasha:** One who has the moon as a crest/light of the moon
19. **Dayalu:** Compassionate one
20. **Devadideva:** God of gods
21. **Dhanadeepa:** Lord of wealth
22. **Dhyanadeepa:** Lord of meditation
23. **Dhyutidhara:** Lord of brilliance
24. **Digambara:** Sky-clad/one who is perceived within oneself
25. **Durjaneeya:** Incomprehensible one
26. **Durjaya:** Unvanquished one
27. **Gangadhara:** Lord of River Ganga
28. **Girijapati:** Consort of Girija
29. **Gunagrahin:** Acceptor of *gunas*/good qualities
30. **Gurudeva:** Supreme guru/God of gurus
31. **Hara:** Destroyer of evil/Remover of sins
32. **Jagadisha:** Master of the Universe
33. **Jaradhishamana:** Redeemer from afflictions
34. **Jatin:** One with matted hair
35. **Kailasha:** One who bestows peace
36. **Kailashadhipati:** Lord of Mount Kailasha
37. **Kailashnatha:** Master of Mount Kailasha
38. **Kamalakshana:** Lotus-eyed lord
39. **Kantha:** Ever-radiant one
40. **Kapalin:** One who wears a necklace of skulls
41. **Kochadaiyaan:** Lord with long dreadlocks/king with matted hair
42. **Kundalin:** One who is adorned with earrings
43. **Lalataksha:** One who has an eye in the forehead

44. **Lingadhyaksha**: Lord of the *lingas*
45. **Lokankara:** Creator of the three worlds
46. **Lokapal**: Protector of the people
47. **Mahabuddhi:** One who is endowed with great intelligence
48. **Mahadeva:** Greatest deity
49. **Mahakala:** One who is beyond time and death
50. **Mahamaya:** Wielder of the worldly illusion
51. **Mahamrityunjaya**: Conqueror of death
52. **Mahanidhi:** Charitable one
53. **Mahashaktimaya:** One of boundless energies
54. **Mahayogi**: Greatest yogi
55. **Mahesha:** Supreme lord
56. **Maheshwara:** Lord of Lords
57. **Nagabhushana**: One who is adorned with serpents
58. **Nataraja:** Lord of dance
59. **Nilakantha:** Blue-throated one
60. **Nityasundara:** Eternally beautiful
61. **Nrityapriya:** Lover of dance
62. **Omkara:** One who has the form of ॐ
63. **Palanhaar:** Protector
64. **Panchatsaran**: Vigorous
65. **Parameshwara:** Supreme god
66. **Paramjyoti:** Radiant one
67. **Pashupati:** Lord of all animals
68. **Pinakin:** One who holds a bow
69. **Pranava:** Controller of the life force/life giver
70. **Priyabhakta:** The favourite of devotees
71. **Priyadarshana:** Of loving vision

72. **Pushkara:** Blue lotus-like/one who provides nourishment
73. **Pushpalochana:** One who has eyes like flowers
74. **Ravilochana:** One who has eyes as bright as the sun
75. **Rudra:** The fearsome one
76. **Sadashiva:** Omnipotent/supreme being/absolute
77. **Sanatana:** Eternal being
78. **Sarvacharya:** Supreme teacher
79. **Sarvashiva:** Eternal lord
80. **Sarvatapana:** Preceptor of all
81. **Sarvayoni:** Source of all
82. **Sarveshwara:** Lord of all
83. **Shambho:** The auspicious one
84. **Shankara:** Destroyer of doubt
85. **Shantah:** Peaceful
86. **Shoolin:** One who has a trident
87. **Shreshtha:** Foremost/ultimate one
88. **Shrikantha:** One who has a pure body
89. **Shrutiprakasha:** Illuminator of the Vedas
90. **Skandaguru:** Preceptor of Skanda
91. **Someshwara:** Lord of the moon
92. **Sukhada:** Giver of joy
93. **Swayambhu:** Self-created
94. **Tejaswani:** One who spreads illumination
95. **Trilochana:** Three-eyed lord
96. **Trilokpati:** Master of all the three worlds
97. **Tripurari:** Destroyer of 'Tripur' (the three cities created by the *asuras*)
98. **Trishulin:** One who has a trident in his hands

99. **Umapati:** Consort of Uma
100. **Vachaspati:** Lord of speech
101. **Vajrahasta:** Wielder of the thunderbolt
102. **Varada:** Bestower of boons
103. **Vedakarta:** Originator of the Vedas
104. **Veerabhadra:** Supreme lord of the nether world
105. **Vishalaksha:** Wide-eyed lord
106. **Vishveshwara:** Lord of the Universe
107. **Vishwanath:** Master of the Universe
108. **Vrishavahana:** One who has a bull as his vehicle

# GLOSSARY

## CHARACTERS

**Ahalya:** Rishi Gautama's wife.

**Arjuna:** Arjuna is the third Pandava brother, son of King Pandu and Queen Kunti. One of the main protagonists of the Mahabharata, he is the spiritual son of Indra, the king of the *devas*.

**Bhagiratha:** One of the most notable kings of Chandravansha (Ikshavaku dynasty). Rama's forefather. Best known for bringing the sacred Ganga down from heaven to the earth by performing severe penance.

**Bhima:** Bhima is the second son of King Pandu and Queen Kunti. He is well known for his strength and his skill with the mace. Born of an incantation by Queen Kunti, given to her by Sage Durvasa, Bhima's celestial father is Vayu, the God of Wind.

**Bhimasura:** Kumbhakarna and Karkati's son.

**Chandrasena:** Ruler of Ujjain. Also known as Avantikapuri, Ujjain was the capital city of the small kingdom of Avanti. In the *Puranas*, it stands as a focal point for spirituality, science, art, ethics, culture, and the scholarly study of holy scriptures, causes championed by the king, who was both devout and deeply knowledgeable about the sacred texts. Scholars, students and devotees from distant places would journey to his realm, seeking knowledge, spiritual guidance and self-exploration.

**Daksha Prajapati:** Son of Brahma and father of Sati, Lord Shiva's wife.

**Dakshina:** The wife of King Kamarupeshwara, and an ardent devotee of Lord Shiva.

**Daruk:** An *asura* and Daruka's husband.

**Daruka:** An *asura* and Daruk's wife, and ardent devotee of Goddess Parvati.

**Dharma:** Son of Lord Brahma, father of the twins Nara and Narayana, avatars of Lord Vishnu.

**Dushan:** *Asura.*

**Ganesha:** The elephant-headed deity who is the son of Shiva and Parvati. Ganesha is venerated as the remover of obstacles, patron of arts and sciences, and the God of Intellect and Wisdom. Ganesha is always honoured at the beginning of all Hindu rites and ceremonies.

**Ganga:** Granddaughter of Lord Brahma, and daughter of Himavat. She is married to King Shantanu of the Kuru dynasty and she resides in the matted tresses of Lord Shiva.

**Garuda:** The king of birds, who is Lord Vishnu's preferred *vahana*. Garuda is worshipped as an independent deity in Hinduism, Buddhism and Jainism.

**Grishna:** Devotee of Lord Shiva. Second wife of Sudharma, and sister of Sudheha. Also called Dhushma/Ghushma.

**Hanuman:** Son of Anjana and Kesari. Hanuman's spiritual father is Vayu, the God of Wind. Hanuman is an ardent devotee of Rama.

**Kaal Bhairava**: Powerful manifestation/avatar of Shiva. Also worshipped in Buddhism.

**Kamarupeshwara:** Ardent devotee of Mahadeva.

**Karkati:** Mother of Bhimasura.

**Kartikeya:** Also known as Skanda, Murugan and Subramanya, Kartikeya is the elder son of Lord Shiva and Goddess Parvati. He is revered as the God of War.

**Kumbhakarna:** Younger brother of Ravana.

**Lakshmana:** Son of King Dasharatha of Ayodhya, born of his second wife, Sumitra. Lord Rama's loyal and favourite brother.

**Lord Brahma:** The Creator in the Hindu holy Trinity.

**Lord Krishna**: Eighth avatar of Vishnu; supreme deity in his own right; ruler of the Yadava clan.

**Lord Shiva:** The Destroyer in the Hindu holy Trinity.

**Lord Vishnu:** The Preserver in the Hindu holy Trinity.

**Mandhata**: One of the most notable kings of Suryavansha (Ikshavaku dynasty). Rama's forefather. Also prominent in Buddhist literature.

**Murti:** Mother of Nara and Narayana, Lord Vishnu's fourth avatars.

**Nakula:** The elder of the twins that Queen Madri, King Pandu's second wife, begets through the incantation taught to her by Queen Kunti. His father is one of the Ashwini Kumara twins.

**Nara:** Lord Vishnu's fourth avatar. Narayana's twin.
**Narada Muni:** Fervent devotee of Lord Vishnu. Vedic sage who travels through the worlds singing the Lord's praises, and causing mischief wherever he goes.
**Narayana:** Lord Vishnu's fourth avatar. Nara's twin.
**Parvati:** Lord Shiva's consort.
**Ravana:** *Asura* king of Lanka. Also a well-known scholar and a devout Shiva-*bhakta*.
**Rishi Atri:** One of the *saptarishis*; son of Lord Brahma and husband of Anusuya. He is the father of Somaraj.
**Rishi Bharadwaja:** Son of Brihaspati and Tara. He is also the father of Dronacharya, the guru of the Pandavas and Kauravas in the Mahabharata.
**Rishi Brihaspati:** Husband of Tara and the chief priest of the *devas*. Commonly referred to as the planet Jupiter.
**Rishi Gautama:** One of the *saptarishis*, son of Lord Brahma. He is married to Ahalya.
**Rishi Kapila:** Grandson of Brahma.
**Rishi Sandipani:** Krishna and Balarama's guru.
**Rohini:** Daksha Prajapati's daughter and Somaraj's favourite wife.
**Sage Agastya:** Sage born of a *yagna* performed by Varuna Deva.
**Sage Aursh:** Son of Urva, grandson of Rishi Bhrigu.
**Sage Suta:** Disciple of Shukadeva, who is the son of Sage Vyasa and the narrator of the *Srimada Bhagavatam*. Sage Suta-ji narrates the origin of the *jyotirlingas* to other sages in the *Shiva Purana*.

**Sahadeva:** Sahadeva is the younger of the twins that Queen Madri, King Pandu's second wife, begets as a result of the incantation taught to her by Queen Kunti. His father is one of the Ashwini Kumara twins.

**Sheshanaga:** Many-headed king of all serpents, on which Lord Vishnu rests in the Kshirasagara. Also referred to as Ananta-Shesha or Adhishesham. According to the Mahabharata, Sheshanaga is said to be born of the union between Sage Kashyapa and his wife, Kadru.

**Shri Rama:** The seventh avatar of Lord Vishnu. Son of King Dasharatha of Ayodhya with his first wife, Kaushalya. He was one of the most notable kings of the Suryavansha (Ikshavaku dynasty).

**Sita:** Wife of Rama, mother of the twins Luv and Kush. Bhudevi or Mother Earth is the spiritual mother of Sita, and her parents are King Janaka and Queen Sunayana of the kingdom of Mithila.

**Somaraj:** Chandra, God of the Moon.

**Sri Adi Shankaracharya:** Great Indian philosopher and saint.

**Sudharma:** Husband of Grishna/Dhushma/Ghushma and Sudheha.

**Sudheha:** Sudharma's first wife and Grishna's sister.

**Sugriva:** Ruler of the *vanara* kingdom of Kishkindha. He was the younger brother of Vali. Born of the union between Surya and Vriksharaja.

**Sumeru:** Sacred five-peaked mountain that is considered to be the centre of the Universe in Hinduism, Buddhism and Jainism.

**Supriya:** Ardent devotee of Lord Shiva.
**Tara:** Wife of Rishi Brihaspati. She begets a son from her union with Somaraj, resulting in the birth of Budh, commonly referred to as the planet Mercury.
**Vali:** Sugriva's elder brother; a *vanara* king.
**Varuna:** The God of Sea and Rain.
**Vindhya:** Mountain range that runs along the west-central part of the Indian subcontinent.
**Yudhishthira:** The eldest son of King Pandu and Queen Kunti. He was the king of Hastinapur and Indraprastha. Yudhishthira's spiritual father is Yama or Dharma, the God of Death.

## WORDS

***Adipurusha:*** The first man.
***Antalstambha*:** Pillar of fire.
***Ashram*:** Humble dwellings of *rishis*. Frequently also occupied by their disciples, who resided with them to glean wisdom from ancient texts and teachings.
***Asura/Daitya*:** Demon.
***Brahmin-hatya*:** The sinful act of killing a brahmin.
***Deva*:** God.
***Dwapara Yuga*:** Third of the four *yugas* or ages mentioned in the ancient Hindu scriptures. The *dwapara yuga* is said to have lasted 2,592 years and is referred to as the Bronze Age.
***Gau-hatya*:** The sinful act of killing a cow.

***Gopuram***: Ornate, monumental entrance tower of a Hindu temple, in southern Indian architecture.
***Kali Yuga***: Fourth of the four *yugas* or ages mentioned in the ancient Hindu scriptures. The *Kali yuga* is said to last 1,296 years and is referred to as the Iron Age.
***Kalpa***: One day of Brahma or 4,320,000,000 human years (4 billion 320 million human years).
***Lingam***: A divine and spiritual structure symbolizing Lord Shiva Himself, the *lingam* typically takes the shape of a phallus. It serves as an abstract or aniconic representation of the deity, believed to be self-manifested and imbued with concentrated energy.
***Loka***: A planet, the Universe, a plane, or a realm of existence.
***Mahamrityunjaya Mantra***: Also referred to as the *Trayambakam Mantra*, translates to 'the great death-conquering mantra'. A verse of the *Rig Veda*, the mantra is addressed to Trayambaka, the Three-eyed One, yet another epithet of Lord Shiva. Chanted to ward off untimely death, and during meditation and prayers to remember the Lord.
***Manava***: Man/human being.
***Mandhata***: One of the most notable kings of the Raghuvansha line of the Suryavansha dynasty. Rama's forefather. Also prominent in Buddhist literature.
***Mukti***: Salvation.
***Patala Loka***: Hell; the abode of the *asuras*.
***Prabhas Patan***: Saurashtra region of Gujarat where the Somnath Temple is situated.

***Pralay***: Dissolution of the Universe at the end of Brahma's day; catastrophic event.

***Rishi***: A sage or saint.

***Saptarishi***: Seven sages including Rishi Agastya, Rishi Atri, Rishi Vashishta, Rishi Vishwamitra, Rishi Gautama, Rishi Jamadagni and Rishi Bharadwaja. They are considered to be the sons of Lord Brahma, and renowned for their spiritual and yogic powers. They have been referred to and have played pivotal roles in the ancient epics of Ramayana and Mahabharata as well (some Upanishads also include Rishi Kashyapa).

***Satya Yuga***: First of the four *yugas* or ages mentioned in the ancient Hindu scriptures. The *satya yuga* is said to last 5,184 years and is referred to as the Golden Age.

***Shaktipeetha***: Meaning 'seat of power', these are places of worship dedicated to Goddess Shakti or Sati, wife of Shiva.

***Shveta Varah Kalpa***: Present day of Brahma that we are currently experiencing.

***Skanda Purana:*** Largest *Purana*, named after Skanda, son of Shiva and Parvati; the text encompasses more than 81,000 verses.

***Swarga Loka***: Heaven; the abode of the *devas*.

***Treta Yuga***: Second of the four *yugas* or ages mentioned in the ancient Hindu scriptures. The *treta yuga* is said to last 3,888 years and is referred to as the Silver Age.

***Trishul***: Lord Shiva's weapon, the trident that He carries.

***Vanavas***: Exile into the forest. For example, in the Mahabharata, after losing a game of dice to the Kauravas, the Pandava brothers were exiled to the forest for a period of twelve years, and in the Ramayana, granting Queen Kaikeyi's boon, King Dasharatha was compelled to exile Rama to the forest for fourteen years.

***Yagna***: Offerings or sacrifices made to the *devas* according to the rites prescribed in the scriptures.

# VISITORS' GUIDE TO THE JYOTIRLINGAS

Planning to visit the sites of the *jyotirlingas*? Here is essential information at a glance!

1. **Somnath, Gujarat**
   **Location:** Somnath Mandir Road, Somnath, Prabhas Patan, Veraval, Gujarat 362268; **Nearest Airport:** Diu (85 km); Porbandar Airport (120 km); **Nearest Railway Station:** Veraval (7 km); **Celebrations:** Shravan month, Shivaratri, Kartik Purnima Fair, Somnath Sthapana Divas (11 May); **Entry Timings:** 6 a.m. to 10 p.m.; **Related Sites:** Parashurama Temple (Lord Shiva relieved Parashurama of his curse), Bhidbhanjan Mahadev Temple, Kamnath Mahadev Temple, Prabhas Patan Museum

2. **Mallikarjuna, Andhra Pradesh**
   **Location:** Srisaila Devasthanam, Srisailam 518101, Kurnool district, Andhra Pradesh; **Nearest Airport:** Rajiv Gandhi International Airport, Hyderabad (250 km); **Nearest Railway Station:** Markapur Road (85 km); **Celebrations:** Mahashivaratri, Ugadi celebrations (Goddess Bhramarambha, Lord Shiva's consort, is worshipped), Sankranti Utsavams, Arudrotsavam,

Sravanamasotsavams, Kartika Masotsavams; **Entry Timings:** 6 a.m. to 3.30 p.m., 6 p.m. to 9 p.m.; **Related Sites:** Hatakeswara Temple, Akkamahadevi Caves (dedicated to Lord Shiva), Shikaresvara Temple, Bhramarambha Devi Temple (related to Goddess Parvati), Lingala Gattu, Istakameswari Temple (dedicated to Goddess Parvati)

3. **Mahakaleshwar, Madhya Pradesh**
   **Location:** 5QM9+58C, inside Mahankal Mandir, Jaisinghpura, Ujjain, Madhya Pradesh 456001; **Nearest Airport:** Devi Ahilyabai Holkar Airport, Indore (53 km); **Railway Station:** Ujjain (2 km); **Celebrations:** Mahashivaratri, Harihara Milan, Sawari, Nitya Yatra, Rang Panchmi (Similar to Holi, prayers are offered to Lord Shiva), Mahashivratri, Shravan month, Nag Panchmi, Kartik Purnima; **Entry Timings:** 4 a.m. to 11 p.m.; **Related Sites:** Kaal Bhairava Temple, Mangalnath Temple

4. **Omkareshwar, Madhya Pradesh**
   **Location:** 65V5 J7, Omkar Ji, Omkareshwar, Mandhata (near Khandawa), Madhya Pradesh 451115; **Nearest Airport:** Indore (75 km); **Nearest Railway Station:** Omkareshwar (12 km); **Celebrations:** Mahashivaratri; **Entry Timings:** 5 a.m. to 9.30 p.m.; **Related Sites:** Siddhanta Temple, Gauri Somnath Temple, Mamleshwar Temple, Kedareshwar Temple

5. **Kedareshwar, Uttarakhand**
   **Location:** Rudraprayag District, Uttarakhand 246445; **Nearest Airport:** Jolly Grant Airport, Dehradun (239 km); **Nearest Railway Station:** Rishikesh (216 km); **Celebrations:** Mahashivaratri, Badri Kedar Festival, Shravani Annakoot festival (Grains are offered to Lord Shiva to be purified); **Entry Timings:** 4 a.m. to 8 p.m.; **Related sites:** Bhairava

Temple, Gaurikund (associated with Parvati and Shiva), Triyuginarayan Temple, Vishwanath Temple - Guptkashi

6. **Bhimashankar, Maharashtra**
**Location:** Bhorgiri village, Khed Taluka, Pune, Maharashtra 410509; **Nearest Airport:** Pune (125 km); **Nearest Railway Station:** Pune (125 km); **Celebrations:** Mahashivaratri, Kartik Purnima; **Entry Timings:** 4.30 a.m. to 9.30 p.m.; **Related Sites:** Gupt Bhimashankar

7. **Vishweshwar, Uttar Pradesh**
**Location:** Sri Kashi Vishwanath Temple, Lahori Tola, Varanasi, Domari, Uttar Pradesh 221001; **Nearest Airport:** Lal Bahadur Shastri Airport (Babatpur Airport/Varanasi Airport) (26–30 km); **Nearest Railway Station:** Varanasi Junction (4.4 km); **Celebrations:** Mahashivaratri, Rangbhari (Aamlaki) Ekadashi, Annakoot, Makar Sankranti, Shravan Maah, Akshaya Tritiya; **Entry Timings:** 3 a.m. to 11 p.m. with few closures for special *aarti*; **Related sites:** Mandhateshwar Temple, Kaal Bhairava Temple, Mrityunjay Mahadev Temple, New Vishwanath Temple

8. **Trayambakeshwar, Maharashtra**
**Location:** Trimbak, Nashik District, Maharashtra 422212; **Nearest Airport:** Nashik Airport (24 km approx.); **Nearest Railway Station:** Nashik Road (40 km); **Celebrations:** Mahashivaratri, Kartik Purnima, Palki Sohala, Shravan month, Kaal Bhairava Jayanti; **Entry Timings:** 5.30 a.m. to 9 p.m.; **Other Related Sites:** Muktidham, Gorakhnath Gufa, Shiv Jata Temple, Someshwar Temple

9. **Baidyanath, Jharkhand**
**Location:** Shankar Road, Bidyanath Lane, Shivganga Mohalla, Deoghar, Jharkhand; **Nearest Airport:** Deoghar

Airport (12 km); **Nearest Railway Station:** Jaisidih (6 km); **Celebrations:** Mahashivaratri, Shravan Mela; **Entry Timings:** 4 a.m. to 9 p.m.; **Related Sites:** Trikutachal Mahadeva Temple, Harla Jori, Baba Basukinath Dham, Shivganga (holy pond)

10. **Nageshwar, Gujarat**
    **Location:** Daarukavanam, Gujarat 361345; **Nearest Airport:** Porbandar (107 km); **Nearest Railway Station:** Dwarka (18 km); **Celebrations:** Mahashivratri, Shravan month, Kartik Purnima; **Entry Timings:** 6 a.m. to 9 p.m.; **Related Sites:** Bhadkeshwar Mahadev Temple, Gomti Ghat temples (dedicated to various gods including Shiva), Siddheshwar Mahadev Temple

11. **Rameshwar, Tamil Nadu**
    **Location:** Rameswaram, Tamil Nadu 623526; **Nearest Airport:** Madurai International Airport (179 km); **Nearest Railway Station:** Rameswaram Railway Station (1 km); **Celebrations:** Mahashivaratri, Aarudra Darsanam, Ramalinga Pratishtha, Thirukalyanam; **Entry Timings:** 5 a.m. to 9 p.m.; **Related Sites:** Agniteertham

12. **Grishneshwar, Aurangabad**
    **Location:** Grishneshwar Temple Road, Verul, Aurangabad, Maharashtra, 431102; **Nearest Airport:** Aurangabad (29 km); **Nearest Railway Station:** Aurangabad (11 km); **Celebrations:** Mahashivaratri, Kartik Purnima, Shravan month; **Entry Timings:** 5.30 a.m. to 9.30 p.m.; **Related Sites:** Kailasha Temple

**NOTE:** All distances are approximate; The visiting hours of all the temples may vary according to occasions (e.g., Mahashivaratri) or due to weather concerns (e.g., in Kedarnath).

# AUTHOR'S NOTE

I have been captivated and inspired by Indian mythology for as long as I can remember. This enduring fascination can be attributed to my grandmother, who would narrate these age-old tales to me when I was younger (and she still does!). This was pivotal in the formation of my indelible connection to the rich tapestry of my cultural legacy.

This abiding interest was further nurtured by my mother from a very young age, who, to this day, orchestrates meticulous plans for our journeys across the vast expanses of India to visit sites of sacred and spiritual beliefs as well as historical and mythological significance. While she enjoys the serenity of the former, I enjoy the mysteries of the latter. A win-win, I'd say, making us the perfect travel partners! Together, we embark on travels to the most ancient temples and holy sites, and the aspiration to visit all the *jyotirlingas* has occupied a prominent place on our shared travel bucket list.

My affinity for all things bibliophilic, and specifically Indian mythological and historical literature, has opened the doors to the enchanting world of my rich history and heritage. In my travels with my mother, I find myself prompted by contemplation, sparking a curiosity about the mythical tales that breathe life into the monumental structures and architectural wonders. I continually research and attempt to establish intricate connections between historical places and facts and mythological narratives, all the while imagining and marvelling at the antiquity of the days past.

My passion for exploring the realms of Indian mythology, delving into the mysteries of temples and unravelling the exquisite stories woven into their sacred walls have become the focal point of my creative aspirations. The desire to rekindle these age-old tales from our ancient scriptures and compile them into a comprehensive collection of stories has emerged as an impassioned endeavour, a pursuit that has always been my dream.

In essence, my intent is to offer a literary haven for those who share a similar curiosity, individuals keen on understanding the impactful legends associated with the places they visit. This venture in finding and retelling stories seeks to guide inquisitive minds, like mine, providing a platform to unearth the cultural and historical treasures encapsulated within the architectural marvels of some of the most ancient temples of India.

With utmost humility and a glint of excitement, I express my gratitude for the spark of interest that ignited within me, the inception of this idea and the opportunity to bring this passion project to life – a vision that began to take form at the height of the COVID-19 pandemic.

I earnestly hope that I have been able to do justice to these marvellous stories that so beautifully unite several Indian epics, scriptures, historical facts and mythological fiction, kindling the curiosity of at least a few readers. My sincere aspiration is to continue this journey in the future, unravelling more tales from our rich cultural tapestry and sharing these profound narratives with each of you.

Thank you for joining me on this exploration.

*Om Namah Shivaya*!

# ACKNOWLEDGEMENTS

I extend my deepest gratitude to the many remarkable individuals whose support and guidance have shaped this journey into the hidden depths of Indian mythology.

Firstly, I am profoundly thankful to my dearest mother and grandmother, for igniting the interest and passion for Indian mythology in me from a very young age. Your vivid storytelling and boundless love for our cultural heritage have shaped the very essence of this book.

I owe a debt of gratitude to the rest of my family. They have not only given me the space and freedom to pursue all of my dreams but have also showered me with endless encouragement to do so. Their warm words have been a constant source of inspiration, celebrating every little and big win along my journey thus far.

I would like to express my gratefulness from the bottom of my heart to my teachers, who allowed me, from a very young age, to slip into the enchanting world of Indian mythology. Whether it was under my desk in the classroom or running off to the library in between classes (and sometimes during!), you will never know how pivotal those memories are to me. Who knew that an interest stemming from all those years ago would culminate with this book in my hands? To this day, they remain some of my biggest cheerleaders and best friends.

I am thankful to the team at Hachette India, for their dedication to this project, making this book a reality.

My sincere appreciation goes to my literary agent, Suhail Mathur of The Book Bakers, for believing in a twenty-two-year-old girl's vision and bringing her childhood dream of becoming a published author to life. Thank you for ever-patiently guiding a first-time author through the intricate nuances of the publishing world. Your championing of my vision for this book has been nothing short of perfect.

My heartfelt appreciation also extends to my closest friends who have known me for a decade and then some, who patiently listen to me speak about this passion of mine and my many other aspirations. Your unrelenting love and affection have been uplifting and a constant source of motivation to me.

Last, but certainly not least, my most heartfelt gratitude to Sri M, whose unwavering presence in my life has profoundly impacted me in ways that extend beyond my comprehension. Your guidance has only blessed and enriched this literary endeavour. Thank you, sir.

Your confidence in me and endless patience have been invaluable.

Thank you, from the depths of my heart.